The Jubilee Poacher

The Jubilee Poacher

Ernest Dobson of Thorpe Hesley & Scholes

Stephen Cooper

Copyright Stephen Cooper, 2018
The right of Stephen Cooper to be identified as Author of this work has been asserted by him in accordance with the Copyright, Designs and Patents Act 1988.
All rights reserved.

ISBN: 1983414360
ISBN 13: 9781983414367

For my friends in Wentworth

"All what you call pot-poaching. It isn't very bad."
(Ernest Dobson, addressing Barnsley magistrates in 1905)

Contents

	List of Illustrations	xi
	Acknowledgements	xiii
	Introduction	xv
One	The Record	1
Two	The Village	38
Three	The Law	62
Four	Attitudes	70
Five	Comparisons	82
	Appendix I: Nets	101
	Appendix II: Guns	103
	Abbreviations & Sources	105
	Other Books by Stephen Cooper	107
	Illustrations	109

List of Illustrations

1	Thorpe Hesley & Scholes, c. 1840	109
2	Wentworth Woodhouse, 2017	110
3	Wentworth from Thorpe Hesley Recreation Ground, 2017	111
4	The Rockingham Mausoleum, by Paul Caton, 2017	112
5	Powerhouse Square, New Yard, Elsecar Workshops, 2017	113
6	The Dove and Dearne canal basin. Elsecar	114
7	Elsecar by the Sea	115
8	Mangham's in Scholes	116
9	Thorncliffe Ironworks	117
10	Hesley Hall, Hesley Lane, 2017	118
11	The Red Lion	119
12	A Pub Outing	120
13	The Ball Inn	121
14	The former Mechanics' Institute, 2017	122
15	Old Methodist Chapel, Thorpe Street, and Sunday School, 1905	123
16	New Methodist Chapel, Thorpe Street	124
17	Barley Hall & Farm	125
18	Thorpe Pit	126
19	Gamekeepers & Poachers, 1885	127
20	Gamekeeper and Poacher, 1912	128

Acknowledgements

I am grateful to my brother Marcus Ashley Cooper for reading and commenting on the text and to my friend Jonathan Addy for many lively discussions about it. I would like to thank my friends Melvyn and Joan Jones for their help with the research; Melvyn for permission to reproduce extracts from his new book *Yorkshire Mining Villages*; and the High Green Archive for permission to reproduce the photos of the Pub Outing, the Red Lion and Thorpe Pit, Barley Hall and Farm, Mangham's Pit at Scholes, Elsecar by the Sea, the Methodist Chapel, Thorpe Street, and the Ball Inn at Hesley Bar. The Rockingham Mausoleum is a drawing by Paul Caton, given to me. Gamekeepers & Poachers, 1885 is from the *Illustrated Sporting & Dramatic News*, reproduced in *The Long Affray;* and Poacher & Gamekeeper, 1912 is a cartoon from *Punch,* again reproduced in *The Long Affray*. The photograph of the old Methodist chapel in Thorpe Street taken in 1905 is from a collection of postcards in the possession of Rotherham City Council Archives Department. All other photographs are from my own collection.

Introduction

When the Census enumerator walked through Scholes in 1861, he had an unusual encounter. Amongst a sea of locals, he met a Swiss lady who came from the village of Corcelles in the canton of Neuchatel. How did she come to be there? We cannot tell; but there she was, with her husband Joseph Dobson, who was a coalminer, a baby (Elmire) and a boy (Ernest) aged 5. Yet, only twenty years previously, the writer John Thomas had compared the misery of Scholes with the splendours of nearby Wentworth Woodhouse [see illustration 2], using the most derogatory terms.

> Houses - not cottages - and these of most Irish aspect, salute the traveller, and bid him remember how closely tacked to the silken skirts of aristocracy is the frieze and worsted of helot labour and poverty. The entrance to Scholes is positively displeasing: if the tastes and habits of the miners dwelling therein demand and require no better accommodation, being the free tenants of an Earl, and breathing the air common to his princely palace, occasion might be taken to give them the liking and use of better habitations.[1]

Perhaps Mrs Dobson had left her native Switzerland (then a poor country) to put on 'the silken skirt', by working at 'the princely palace' in some capacity or

---

1 John Thomas, *Walks in the Neighbourhood of Sheffield*, 1844, cited by Melvyn Jones in *South Yorkshire Mining Villages*, 71.

other? She had undoubtedly married a man from Scholes, whose house resembled a contemporary Irish hovel, and where conditions were seemingly as bad as those endured by Spartan slaves in the 5th century before Christ. We also know that her son was to lead a remarkable, if not wholly successful, life.

I first came across Ernest Dobson in two articles in the *Sheffield Daily Telegraph* and the *Barnsley Chronicle* for Tuesday 2 May 1905, in the British Newspaper Archive. Entitled 'An Old Poaching Hand' (though he was only 49 at the time), these told how he had recently been caught poaching rabbits on Wharncliffe Chase near Wortley, some six miles from Scholes. On this occasion, Dobson admitted his guilt, but sought to justify himself in two ways. First, he said that he hadn't been very successful, since he had "got no rabbits", second he said "all what you call pot-poaching. It isn't very bad." The magistrates were not impressed. Neither excuse was credible. Dobson also made it clear that he would certainly have taken a rabbit or two if he could have done so, and in any case the record showed that he had literally dozens of previous convictions, of which no less than 32 were for poaching. The magistrates duly fined him 40 shillings and costs, which may be considered lenient in the circumstances.

But I had become curious about Ernest Dobson and his poaching and I set out to discover more. It was clear that he had appeared before the courts on numerous occasions; but I did not expect to find that he had become so well-known that in 1887, when he was convicted for the 50th time, he was dubbed 'The Jubilee Poacher', because this was the year of Queen Victoria's Golden Jubilee. Nor did I expect to find that there were prison records showing that Dobson was born in 1856, received an elementary education, was an Anglican, had light brown hair, and was 5 feet 9 inches tall (though sometimes he measured in at 5 feet 10).

I wanted to know more, and I have set out what I discovered about Ernest Dobson's career in chapter I, while in chapter II, I look at his background – where he came from and where he went poaching. In chapter III, I summarise the law which applied at the time. In chapter IV I consider the attitudes to poaching which prevailed at the time, particularly amongst the upper classes. In the last chapter I draw some conclusions as to whether Dobson had a point, when he claimed that he what he did was not 'very bad'.

The Jubilee Poacher

Despite the wealth of information available, Dobson remained and remains a mysterious character. To begin with, there was a puzzle about his age, arising from the fact that the newspapers did not normally give it. When they did (as in 1882), they said he was 21. However, if the information in the Censuses of 1861 and 1871 is correct, he was born in 1856, which would mean that he was actually 26 at the time.

I now think that Dobson either lied in 1882, so as to invite the sympathy of the court, on the grounds of (relative) youth, or that the authorities made a mistake, or were unsure, as to his true age, and put this down as the age of majority (which was 21 at the time). But there remains a puzzle, because we now know that he was only 48 in 1904, when a Sheffield paper carried a report about a court appearance and said that he was 'aged'. The journalist made a mistake; but does this tell us that he had lived a hard life, and looked old? Or that, like the characters in Anton Chekhov's plays, men were then considered 'old' in those days, as soon as they were no longer 'young'. (The other alternative, of course, is that there was more than one man called Ernest Dobson; but that is unlikely).

Whatever the solution to this problem, it is clear that Police and court records were not kept as efficiently in the 19th century as the computer now permits; and the number of convictions recorded by the Rotherham magistrates (before whom he appeared most often) was not the same as that recorded in Barnsley or Sheffield, and certainly differed from the records in Wakefield Prison. So there is a doubt as to the true number of his convictions.

In addition, I have not been able to discover whether Dobson was ever married, and he simply disappears from the records, after 1906. Did he move to another part of the country and assume another name, as it appears that he had done in the 1890s? Or did he simply die at this time? It is extremely unlikely that he would have been killed in the Great War of 1914-18, since he would already have been 58 when the War broke out and would not have been eligible for military service.

Finally I should explain that this book is principally based on local newspapers held by the British Newspaper Archive, though I did also consult The Times Newspaper Archive. Both these sources have the huge advantage that they can be consulted online. I did consult the *Rotherham Advertiser* in Rotherham

Stephen Cooper

Archives, Clifton Lane, Rotherham; but at present this can only be read on microfilm, or via a limited range of newspaper cuttings, which makes the search much more laborious. In addition, the *Advertiser* only appeared once a week during the period I was interested in, so that it is a less fruitful source than the main Sheffield papers.

Stephen Cooper
Thorpe Hesley
South Yorkshire
January 2018

One

The Record

1877

In the summer of 1877 a new church was consecrated in Wentworth - paid for by Earl Fitzwilliam. This was also the moment when Ernest Dobson was first mentioned in the newspapers. His birth certificate shows that he was born nearby in Scholes in 1856, and was still living there at the time of the Censuses taken in 1861 and in 1871. The latter records him as living with his parents and two sisters Elmire (11) and Theresa Celestine (3); and it also tells us that at 42 his mother was three years older than his father, and that she originally came from Switzerland. Dobson was still only 15, but he was already a miner, like his father.

My friends, who know about these things, tell me that Ernest is likely to have started poaching even before he started work. Given that Scholes was situated on the edge of Earl Fitzwilliam's Park at Wentworth, he probably began by going into the local woods and fields. This is certainly what the newspapers tell us that he did when he was older. The *Sheffield Daily Telegraph* printed brief details on Tuesday 12 June; but the fullest report appeared in the weekly *Rotherham Advertiser*, on Saturday 16 June 1877.

Stephen Cooper

ROTHERHAM COURT HOUSE.
WEST RIDING COURT.
DAMAGING UNDERWOOD AT WENTWORTH.

Before Mr. G.W. Chambers (in the chair),[2] Mr. H. Oxter, and Mr. James Montagu. Ernest Dobson, George Gillett, Jacob Cooke, and Henry Walton, all of Scholes, were charged by William Airey, an assistant gamekeeper, in the service of Earl Fitzwilliam[3] with wilful damage to growing underwood. Mr. Packwood prosecuted.

Wm. Airey said that On May 23rd he heard a noise in the Rockingham Wood, Wentworth, and when he went there he saw the defendants. Two of them, Dobson and Gillott, were up some trees, stealing young rooks, and the other two were on the ground ready to receive the birds, as they were thrown down. He went up to them and they got round him, and said that they should not go until they had got what they wanted. One of them (Walton), with a stick which he had in his hand, struck witness with such violence over the arm, that it broke the stick. The damage was laid, nominally, at 1d each, and Mr Packwood stated that they brought the case forward with a view to stopping the intolerable nuisance of persons trespassing in the wood and taking the young birds. The defendants pleaded guilty. Dobson, who had been previously tried three times for game trespasses, was fined 20 shillings, and the costs and the damage, or three weeks' imprisonment; Gillett, Cooke, and Walton were each fined 10s., the costs, and the damage, or ten days' imprisonment; Walton was fined 20s. including costs, or three weeks, for the assault.

---

2 G.W. Chambers is more than likely the same George Wilton Chambers (1812-1904!), whose family owned Chambers and Son, of Masbrough [WD, 1837] and had been involved in the Rotherham boat disaster of 1841, when 50 people, mainly children, drowned.

3 This was the 6th Earl (1815-1902!), whose son William Wentworth-Fitzwilliam, known as Viscount Milton was an epileptic and died in 1877 at the age of 37. A George Airey was listed as living at Mausoleum Lodge Nether Haugh, in 1891: [WD]. The Rockingham Mausoleum itself is also in Wentworth Park [see illustration 4].

Later the same year, Dobson was convicted again, the offence being 'trespass in pursuit of game', and the court does not seem to have been informed of his previous conviction for criminal damage. The *Sheffield Daily Telegraph* and the *Sheffield Independent* for Tuesday 9 October 1877 each carried the story.

ROTHERHAM POLICE COURT. MONDAY.
GAME CASES.

Before Mr. H. Jubb (Chairman)[4] and Mr. W. S. Cadman, Esq., Ernest Dobson, of Scholes (who did not appear), had been summoned by Frederick Airey, of Wentworth, for trespassing in pursuit of game, at Wentworth, on the 30th ult. Mr. Peagam prosecuted.

About three o'clock on the Sunday named Airey and another man named Robinson saw the defendant in Squirrel Wood, with a dog, which he was inciting to follow a rabbit.[5] Complainant spoke to him, and he replied that he had gone into the wood to fetch his dog out. Fined 40s. and costs, or one month's imprisonment.

1878

Dobson's next convictions were for poaching in Scholes Wood, and were reported in the *Sheffield Independent* on Saturday 23 February 1878 and Tuesday 10 December 1878. In the second report Dobson was already described as 'an old offender', though he was still only 22.

---

4   Henry Jubb is listed as a magistrate in 1891 [WD]. He lived in Boston Castle Grove, though Jubb was a common name.

5   The *Independent* has 'urging a dog to catch a rabbit'.

SCHOLES WOOD.
GAME TRESPASS.

Ernest Dobson, Scholes, was charged with trespassing in pursuit of game in Scholes Wood on the 7th inst.. Fined 4s. and costs or two months' imprisonment.

GAME TRESPASS IN SCHOLES WOOD.

Before G. W. Chambers, Esq. (chairman), W. S. Cadman, Esq., and H. Jubb, Esq. Alfred Wood, Thorpe Hesley, was fined 20s. and costs, or one month's imprisonment, for having committed a game trespass in Scholes Wood, on the 27th ult.; and Ernest Dobson, of Thorpe Hesley, who did not appear, and who was an old offender, was committed to prison for two months without the option of a fine. Another man named Kilroy, who was acting with the other men, absconded before the summons could be served on him. Mr. Parker-Rhodes[6] appeared for Earl Fitzwilliam, on whose preserves the offences were committed.

On this occasion the magistrates had sentenced Dobson to imprisonment without the option of a fine; and we know, from an obscure entry in the register of Wakefield Prison, that he was now apprehended and jailed, probably for the first time in his life. The register refers to him as Ernest Dobson, collier of Thorpe Hesley and Scholes, aged 22, and tells us briefly that he was in prison again in 1879, 1880, 1881, and 1882; but no further details are given at this point.

1879

The newspapers tell us of two court appearances this year, both before the Police Court in Rotherham, and both relating to offences committed near Dobson's home; but his fame, or notoriety, was spreading. The first appearance

---

6 Frederick Parker Rhodes later became clerk to the West Riding magistrates in Rotherham. [WD, 1891].

was reported by both the *Sheffield Independent* on Friday 31 January and by the *Barnsley Chronicle* on 1 February 1879:

ROTHERHAM AND NEIGHBOURHOOD.
GAME TRESPASS AT SCHOLES.

At the Rotherham Police Court yesterday, before Ald. Wigfield (Mayor), and Ald. Morgan (ex- Mayor), Ernest Dobson, of Thorpe Hesley, was fined £4 and costs, or four months imprisonment, for having committed two game trespasses on the Earl Fitzwilliam's estate at Scholes, on the 23rd and 25th inst. Defendant had committed a large number of similar offences, and had been often warned. Mr. Parker-Rhodes prosecuted.

The prison register for 1879 tell us that Dobson arrived in Wakefield on 4 March, when he said that he was 23 years old and a collier, that he had received an elementary education, that his religion was 'Church' [of England], and that he had light brown hair. The clerk who completed the register was only aware of four previous convictions. Curiously he was discharged on 3 May but re-admitted the same day, and ultimately discharged on 3 July. The explanation must be that he was committed in the first place for non-payment of the fine imposed by the magistrates at the end of January, and then re-arrested for non-payment of another fine. At any rate, it is clear that prison did not act as a deterrent because he was back before the magistrates within a matter of weeks, as recorded in the *Barnsley Chronicle* for Saturday 13 September 1879:

For game trespass at Thorpe Hesley on land belonging to Earl Fitzwilliam, Ernest Dobson was fined 40s. and costs by the Rotherham Bench.

1880

There were two convictions this year, according to the *Sheffield Daily Telegraph* for Tuesday 31 August 1880 and the *Barnsley Chronicle* for Saturday 4 September 1880,

Stephen Cooper

AN OLD POACHER IN TROUBLE.

Yesterday at the Rotherham Police Court Ernest Dobson, collier, Thorpe Hesley, a well-known poacher, was fined 4s and costs, or two months' imprisonment in default, for having committed offences against the Game Laws on the estate of Earl Fitzwilliam, on the 21th and 25th instant, in Rockingham Wood and Bolderfall Wood. Defendant was found on both occasions demolishing rabbit burrows to procure game. When seen by Police Constable Asherwood he left the wood, but returned as soon as the constable got out of sight. Mr. Parker-Rhodes represented Earl Fitzwilliam.

In each case, the 'victim' here was the 6th Earl Fitzwilliam (1815-1902), grandfather of the better known 7th Earl, who was known as 'Billy Fitzbilly' (1872-1943). This was because, before the coming into force of the Ground Game Act on 7 September 1880, the complainant in cases of poaching was invariably the landowner; and the Earl was the largest of these in the area.

1881

At some date between 1871 and 1881, the Dobson family moved from Scholes to Thorpe Hesley. The Census for 1881 shows them living in Hesley Lane, near Hesley Hall and Hesley Wood [see illustrations 1 & 10] The head of the family is the father, Joseph (aged 48 and a coal miner). The mother's name appears as Laura, but she is clearly the same woman as the Louise of 1871, since she was born in Switzerland. Ernest's name is now spelt 'Earnest', but he is still a coal miner. His younger sister Theresa Celestine is only 12 and at school. Elmire is no longer at home, but then she would now be 20 or 21 and has probably married. There are no lodgers in the household.

In 1881 Ernest Dobson was 26, but he had not learned the error of his ways. He was back before the Rotherham magistrates, and once again for game trespass on the Fitzwilliam estate at Scholes – it is no great distance from Hesley Lane to Scholes; but this time he has also become involved in an assault on a gamekeeper. The *Sheffield Daily Telegraph* for Tuesday 3 May 1881 tells the story.

GAME TRESPASSERS AT SCHOLES AND WENTWORTH.

Yesterday at the Court House, Rotherham, Ernest Dobson, collier, Thorpe Hesley, against whom 16 convictions of game trespass had been recorded since April, 1875, was fined 40s. and costs, one month in default, for trespassing in pursuit of game on the 13th on land at Scholes belonging to Earl Fitzwilliam. He was fined a like penalty with a similar alternative for assaulting George Airezan,[7] an under-keeper, who caught him with his arm up a rabbit hole. He was also fined a third 40s. and costs or a third month's imprisonment in default for trespassing pursuit of conies[8] at Wentworth on land in the occupation of Mr. Redfearn on the 19th April. John Smith, collier, Thorncliffe, was fined 20s., including costs for trespassing at Wentworth with Dobson. In both cases a summons had been issued against a man named Kingston. He did not appear, and a warrant was issued. Mr. F. Parker-Rhodes prosecuted in each case.

We note from the above that the usual sentence imposed on Dobson was a fine, with a term of imprisonment if he did not pay it. Looking at his record as a whole, it appears that he usually failed to pay. This is evident from the following article which appeared in the *Sheffield Daily Telegraph* on Tuesday 20 September 1881 and in the *Barnsley Chronicle* on Saturday 24 September 1881.

FREQUENT OFFENDER AGAINST THE GAME LAWS.

At the Rotherham Court House yesterday, Ernest Dobson, labourer, of Thorpe Hesley pleaded guilty and was fined 40s. and costs or a months' imprisonment for trespassing in pursuit of rabbits on land belonging to Earl Fitzwilliam, on the 8th inst. The defendant recently came out of prison, having served a term for game trespass, which was his sixteenth conviction for that offence. Mr F Parker Rhodes prosecuted.

---

[7] This should be 'Airey'.
[8] Rabbits.

Not all Dobson's convictions were for poaching. It is clear from the following article that he was not like James Harker, who avoided alcohol on the grounds that it made him less effective at his 'work'. The *Sheffield Independent* for Tuesday 25 October and the *Sheffield Daily Telegraph* for Saturday 29 October 1881 reported as follows:

DISGRACEFUL AFFAIR AT THORPE HESLEY.

Yesterday at the Rotherham Court House, Wilfrid Wood[9] and Ernest Dobson, both Thorpe Hesley men, were charged with being drunk and disorderly, on tbe 22nd inst. Dobson was further charged with assaulting Police Sergeant Stringer. The sergeant sought to disperse a number of drunken men who were fighting, among whom were the prisoners. Wood became peaceable after a time, but his condition was such that he had to be locked up. Dobson was very violent and kicked the officer. There were 22 previous convictions against Dobson. He was fined 5s. and costs, or 7 days, for being drunk, and committed for a month for assaulting the police. Wood had been seven times previously convicted, and was fined 5s. and costs.

1882

The next headline indicates a step change in Ernest Dobson's 'career'. He is still poaching close to home, in Smithy Wood, on the Ecclesfield side of Thorpe Hesley; but he now moves from the magistrates' court to the Assizes. The reason is obvious, from the opening lines of the relevant newspaper reports: guns were involved.[10] The *Sheffield Independent*, the *Leeds Times*, and the *Yorkshire Post and Leeds Intelligencer* all carried the news, on Saturday 4 February 1882.

---

9   For Wilfred Wood, see also under 1887 (Jubilee Year).
10 See Appendix II.

POACHING AFFRAY AT ECCLESFIELD.[11]
LEEDS WINTER ASSIZES.

William Barras and Ernest Dobson, labourers, of Ecclesfield, were indicted for unlawfully, with divers other persons unknown, entering enclosed land for the purpose of taking game, they being also armed each with a gun. Mr. Stuart Wortley[12] prosecuted, and Mr. Fenwick defended. Mr. Wortley said that the prisoners were indicted for an offence against the game laws, under a statute which made it a misdemeanour for persons to enter land in the night time, to the number of three or more, with weapons in their hands.

Half an hour after midnight, on the 30th December, the prisoners, in company with two other men not in custody, were in Smithy Wood, Ecclesfield, property of the Duke of Norfolk, but occupied and preserved by Messrs. Newton, Chambers, and Co., Thorncliffe Ironworks.[13] Jesse May and George Poppleton, two keepers, were watching in the wood when they heard the discharge of a gun.[14] They went in the direction of the sound, when they heard some people moving. Soon after the prisoners and two other men came in sight, and Barras fired into a tree in which some pheasants were roosting. The keepers then came in sight, but Dobson kept them at bay by presenting his gun, the other men throwing stones. The keepers had to retire, but not before they had perfectly identified the prisoners. Mr. Fenwick on behalf of his client submitted that it was a case of mistaken identity. The Court adjourned before witnesses had been called.

---

11 For a typical affray see illustration 19.

12 Charles Beilby Stuart-Wortley, 1st Baron Stuart of Wortley PC (1851–1926) was a close relative of the Earl of Wharncliffe. Educated at Rugby School and Balliol College, Oxford, he was called to the bar at Inner Temple in 1876. He was the first Conservative to be elected as MP for Sheffield in 1880, and was elected for the new Sheffield Hallam constituency in 1885. He served under Lord Salisbury as Under-Secretary of State for the Home Department between 1885 and 1886 and again from 1886 to 1892. He was raised to the peerage in 1917.

13 The indictment now refers to the occupier of the land, as well as the landowner, because of the coming into force of the Ground Game Act 1880: see above.

14 George Poppleton of Hesley Lane, Chapeltown was listed as a gamekeeper in 1891 [WD].

The case was duly sent for trial by jury at the Assizes. The *Bradford Daily Telegraph* and the *Leeds Intelligencer* each carried the news on Monday 6 February 1882.

> The business of the Leeds Assizes was resumed at the Town Hall, Leeds, this morning, Wm. Barras (37), on bail, labourer, of Sheffield, and Ernest Dobson, indicted for poaching at night at Ecclesfield on the 30th of December, were again placed at the bar. Mr Stuart Wortley, M.P., prosecuted, and the prisoner Barras was defended by Mr Fenwick.
>
> The case for the prosecution was opened yesterday afternoon, when evidence was given by the gamekeepers to the effect that the prisoners with some others were poaching on the lands of Messrs Newton, Chambers, and Co., Smithy Wood, Ecclesfield, near Sheffield, the land being owned by the Duke of Norfolk. The prisoners, it was alleged by the prosecutors, were on the land armed, but this morning Mr Fenwick on the part of the prisoners called a witness who stated that the prisoner Barras lodged with her at Sheffield, and on the night in question he came home early and remained in bed all the night. The prisoner Dobson called a witness who swore that the prisoner was in his house smoking and drinking. His Lordship summed up some length, and the jury retired to consider the verdict. After lengthy consultation the jury found the prisoners guilty, and his Lordship sentenced Barras to six months, and Dobson to twelve months' imprisonment.

This was the heaviest sentence of imprisonment Ernest Dobson ever received.

The Wakefield prison register does not mention a date for his discharge, so we must assume that he served the full twelve months.

1883

In 1883 there was something new to report about Ernest Dobson. The *Sheffield Daily Telegraph* for Monday 2 April 1883 and the *Liverpool Mercury* carried the following story:

The Jubilee Poacher

Edward Dobson, a miner at Thorpe Hesley, made his escape from the West Riding police office, at Rotherham, on Saturday. He had been convicted of poaching in the borough, and was awaiting trial for another poaching offence by the West Riding justices. Dobson is noted as a fleet runner and but for his poaching propensities would have been taken up by sporting men as a professional pedestrian.

If this is right it means that Dobson had re-offended almost immediately, after being sentenced to 12 months in 1882. Further, we learn from the Wakefield Prison Register that he served three consecutive sentences of one month, between April and June 1883. The *Barnsley Chronicle* for Saturday 30 June tells us that Dobson had taken to going a little further away from home, possibly in an attempt to escape detection.

POACHING AT WORTLEY.

A well-known poacher named Ernest Dobson, who resides at Thorpe Healey, was charged with trespassing in pursuit of conies on the 9th March last at Wortley. Defendant who had only just been apprehended on his leaving Wakefield gaol, pleaded guilty, and wished the Bench to hear the case. Mr J. Carrington, who prosecuted, said defendant and another man were found in search of conies. He had no witnesses present, but as defendant pleaded guilty he had no objection to the Bench hearing the case. It appeared that defendant had just finished a term of three months' imprisonment. In April last he escaped from the police at Rotherham, and on being captured was lodged in gaol. He was fined 20s. and costs for the offence; defendant stated that he was tired of being in prison.

1886

As far as we know Ernest Dobson kept out of trouble for a time; but he was back before the courts in 1886, according to the *Sheffield Independent* for Tuesday 7 December and Saturday 11 December that year.

ROTHERHAM WEST RIDING POLICE COURT. MONDAY.
GAME TRESPASS.

Ernest Dobson, labourer, was charged with trespassing in search of game on land in the occupation of Mr. Joseph Pilley,[15] between Thorpe Hesley and Wentworth, on Nov. 22nd. Mr. Hickmott prosecuted on behalf of Earl Fitzwilliam. Evidence was given showing that the defendant had encouraged his dogs to pursue hares, and threatened an under-keeper named Wood. Fined 40s. and costs, or one month's imprisonment.

1887

Queen Victoria's Golden Jubilee fell on 20 June 1887, when Ernest Dobson was only 31; but he achieved a record of his own that year, though one would not know it from the newspaper reports which appeared at the time. The *Sheffield Daily Telegraph* 4 May and the *Sheffield Independent* for 7 May 1887 reported as follows.

SHEFFIELD TOWN HALL.
WEST RIDING COURT.

Ernest Dobson, labourer, of Thorpe Hesley, Thos. O'Donnell, miner, and Joseph Barras moulder, both of Chapeltown[16] were summoned for trespassing in pursuit of game on land belonging to the Duke of Norfolk at Thorpe Hesley Park on the 20th ult. Two of the defendants were seen by a gamekeeper digging rabbit burrows, while Barrow the third, it was alleged, kept watch on the road, and at the keeper's approach held up his hands as a signal to his companions. The case against Barras was dismissed, Dobson was fined £2. 7s 9d including costs, or in default to be imprisoned for one month with hard la-

---

15 Joseph Pilley is listed as a farmer and builder, living in Hesley Lane, in 1891(WD). This is an example of the way in which the Ground Game Act of 1880 had changed the law: see chapter III.
16 Throughout this book, the Chapeltown referred to is the one near Sheffield, not the one near Leeds.

bour, O'Donnell was fined 15s. 6d., or in default to be imprisoned for seven days with hard labour. Wilfred Wood, miner, Thorpe Hesley, was fined 14s. 6d., or be imprisoned for seven days with hard labour for a similar offence at Thorpe Hesley, on the 23rd ult. Mr. Wightman prosecuted in all cases.

The *Sheffield Evening Telegraph* for Tuesday 20 December and the *Sheffield Independent* for Wednesday 21 December 1887 carried the following article:

HIS 42ND CONVICTION.

Ernest Dobson, collier, Hesley lane, of Chapeltown, was charged on a warrant with having assaulted Henry Horsley, Ecclesfield, the 12th October. Prisoner and complainant were at the Travellers Inn, when without any provocation, prisoner knocked Horsley down and seriously assaulted him, knocking three of his teeth out. Prisoner admitted that he "gave Horsley a bit with his boot". Superintendent Midgley said prisoner had been before the court 41 times, chiefly for poaching and assaults on the police. His last conviction was in July of the present year. The Bench committed him to prison for one month with hard labour.

We note that there is nothing here about Dobson's being known as 'The Jubilee Poacher'; and indeed the magistrates seem to have thought that he had only been convicted some 40 times, not 50. We have to wait some two years for the soubriquet to be attached.

1888

At the end of 1888, the long arm of the law caught up with Dobson once again, only for him to escape it. The *Sheffield Independent* for Tuesday 4 December 1888 explains.

ROTHERHAM WEST RIDING POLICE COURT, MONDAY.
A BATCH OF POACHERS.

Oswald Wragg and Enoch Swift were charged with game trespass, November 20th, on the estate of Earl Fitwilliam. Wragg had been convicted 28 times, four times in 1888, for game trespass. Swift had been convicted 23 times, twice in 1888. Fined 40s. each and costs. Enoch Swift was further fined 20s. and costs, for game trespass on November 26th, on land in the occupation of William Senior, situated between Thorpe and Wentworth.[17] He was seen with two men named Alfred Linley and Ernest Dobson, by Adams, Parker, Robinson, and Sales from a wood near. Swift and the other men were beating, and Dobson shot a hare. They then ran away. Linley and Dobson had since disappeared from their homes at Thorpe, and a warrant was issued for their apprehension.

1890

When he started his career in poaching, Ernest Dobson was young and he confined himself to poaching close to home – in Scholes Wood, Squirrel Wood and Rockingham Wood, for example. As he got older, he went further afield, to Smithy Wood, Chapeltown, Wortley Park and Wharncliffe Chase. As far as we know, the furthest he went was into the countryside adjoining Pontefract, and the neighbouring counties of Derbyshire and Nottinghamshire. He would usually go out at night, often, we may suppose on a moonlit night. Sometimes he went alone, sometimes with a friend, and sometimes in a gang; but whenever and wherever he went, there was a risk of violence being done, and not just to rabbits and birds.

At the beginning of 1890 Dobson became involved in an alarming fight with a local gamekeeper keeper, and allegedly threatened to kill him afterwards. The reports which appeared in the *Sheffield Evening Telegraph* on Tuesday 18 February 1890 and in the *Sheffield Daily Telegraph* and the *Sheffield Independent* on Wednesday 19th February may surprise those who think that the common man could not expect to receive justice at the hands of the magistrates.

---

17 William Senior is listed as a carter in 1891 in Wentworth [WD]; but it was a common name.

THE "JUBILEE POACHER" IN TROUBLE AGAIN.
ASSAULTING AND THREATENING TO MURDER A KEEPER.

The West Riding Court of the Sheffield Town Hall, yesterday, before Mr. F. W. Bagshawe[18] and Mr. W. T. W. Cadman. Ernest Dobson, collier, of Hesley lane, Chapeltown, was charged with assaulting and threatening Timothy Weatherall, gamekeeper, in the employ of Messrs. Newton Chambers, and Co., on the 15th instant.[19] Mr. D. Wightman, who appeared for the prosecutor, said the prisoner had been charged a number of times with poaching, and in the Jubilee year was summoned and convicted for the 50th time in that and other courts, mostly for game offences. He now went under the title the "Jubilee Poacher," but unfortunately this case was much more serious one than poaching. The man was caught poaching on Saturday, but was not summoned for that, as his subsequent conduct amounted to a much more serious matter. He was charged with assaulting the keeper, and subsequently using threats to shoot him, which induced him to believe that he was in danger of his life from the violence of the prisoner.

Weatherall was keeper over Hesley Park and Smithy Wood, and Saturday afternoon, about 2.30, he was in the latter and found the man poaching. He told him that he was at his old game again, and asked him to leave the wood. They walked on for a distance, when without any warning Dobson suddenly struck the keeper in the face with his fist. They struggled together for some time, and eventually separated. Prisoner then picked up a piece of brick and struck him in the face with it, causing the blood to flow. They struggled again on the ground, and the prisoner threatened what he would do, amongst other things saying

---

18 Francis Westby Bagshawe M.A. D.L., J.P. was chairman of the petty sessions in Eckington, as well as being one of the West Riding magistrates. He lived at The Oaks, in Norton, Sheffield, which was owned by his family between 1699 and 1987 [WD]. This is now Oakes Park, and is a Christian holiday centre for young people.

19 According to the *Sheffield Independent*, Weatherall was keeper for Mr. A. M. Chambers and Mr. T. C. Newton, and other gentlemen, rather than simply for 'Newton, Chambers & Co.' He lived in Smithy Wood. Pepper's Inn was *The Travellers*, in Hesley Wood: [WD, 1891].

that he would a blow hole through him before the night was out. When they got up he struck Weatherall with a stick on the head, and they again went down together, Dobson being on the top.

One of them cried for assistance. An innkeeper named Pepper, who lives near, heard this, and on going in the wood saw the men down, and the prisoner with a piece of brick his hand. He took the brick away, and the men continued struggling. After they separated, Dobson again struck the keeper in the face twice, and picking up a stick threatened what would do. They fought again, and Weatherall at last struck Dobson on the head with his stick. Prisoner said he had as much right in the wood as the keeper or his master either and refused to leave, and Weatherall left him instead of insisting on his going out of the wood. The keeper was badly hurt about the face, and still suffered pain from the prisoner attempting to gouge out his eye.

In the evening Dobson got a gun and went to Pepper's inn, where he said "Bring me a glass of beer; it's the last shall have, as I am going to blow a hole through Weatherall to-night." Pepper took the gun from him, and like a sensible man, took it to the back door and fired it off. [Dobson] got back the gun and re-loaded it, and repeated his threats to shoot Weatherall. He called out for another glass of beer, saying, "It's the last I shall have. If I don't shoot him to-night, I hope the Lord will paralyse me."

The prosecutor and other witnesses gave evidence in support of this statement. Prisoner contended that he was not poaching, and that he was assaulted several times by the keeper before retaliating. He got his temper rather high, and they had a bit of a battle.

Corroborative testimony was also given by William Pepper, Sergeant Plowright and George Knott, pit sinker, Cowley Hill. They said that the prisoner had a wound on the side of his head, and said that Weatherall had allowed his dog to bite him, and furthermore that he had struck the first blow. This helps to explain the decision of the magistrates, to treat Ernest Dobson very leniently:

Mr. Bagshawe said the prisoner would be bound over—himself in £10 and to find three sureties of each—to the peace for 12 months, or in default to prison for two months with hard labour. As regards the assault the magistrates considered that after the view they had taken of the other charge [i.e. the poaching itself] it was not necessary to inflict any further punishment, especially since there was some discrepancy in the evidence as to how the assault was committed. There was no one present when it began, and they had therefore no evidence as to that, except the statements made by the prisoner and the prosecutor.

On the other hand, the court thought that the conduct of the prisoner in going to public house and using threatening language after the affray was 'very reprehensible'.

Within a few weeks Dobson was back before a different Bench. The incident was reported in the *Sheffield Independent* on Thursday 17 April 1890.

FOND OF EARL OF WHARNCLIFFE'S CONIES.
BARNSLEY POLICE COURT.

Ernest Dobson, miner, of Chapeltown, appeared to answer a summons, charging him with having trespassed on land belonging to the Earl of Wharncliffe, at Wortley, on the 24th of December last. Mr. Carrington prosecuted. Christopher Parkin, a game watcher,[20] deposed to seeing defendant ranging about Wharncliffe Chase for fully two hours with a stick in his hand. Witness went up to him, and found two rabbits in his pocket and one in his hand. The Chairman said it was defendant's 29th appearance at various courts in Yorkshire. He had been fined 20s., 30s., and 40s, in addition to two months imprisonment. He would be fined 20s. and costs, or one month in default.

---

20 According to the Census of 1891 Christopher Parkin, aged 43, and born in Thurgoland, was a park keeper who lived at Wharncliffe Lodge, on the Chase itself. He was married with two children aged 16 and 13: ancestry.co.uk.

The newspaper reports are beginning to make it clear that Dobson was well known to local gamekeepers, which led to frequent arrests and prosecutions; but the journalists did not always get their facts right. We learn from the Wakefield Prison Register that Dobson was admitted there on 16 April 1890 and that this was because he had been fined by the Barnsley Magistrates, and ordered to spend 28 days in prison (rather than one or two months), if he failed to pay.

The above was not the last time that Dobson was convicted in 1890. He offended again on 15 May and appeared before the Sheffield magistrates soon after. The *Sheffield Evening Telegraph* for Tuesday 27 May 1890 and the *Sheffield Daily Telegraph* for Wednesday 28 May 1890 each reported:

SHEFFIELD TOWN HALL.
WEST RIDING COURT.
HEAVY FINE FOR GAME TRESPASS.

Ernest Dobson miner, Thorpe Hesley, and Oswald Wragg, miner, were summoned for trespassing in search of game on land in Grange Lane, over which Mr. Michael Ellison has the right to shoot, on May 15.[21] Dobson, who did not appear, was also charged with a similar offence committed on the same land, and other land occupied by Messrs. Newton and Chambers, on the 19th inst. Mr. D. Wightman, who appeared for the prosecution, stated that the defendants were persistent poachers, who set game preservers, gamekeepers, and the Bench at defiance. Sending them to prison had no effect upon them, and by a night's poaching they could easily obtain money to pay any fine magistrates could inflict upon them. Dobson was a small annuity to him (Mr. Wightman), as he had been employed to prosecute him on many occasions. He made his 50th appearance in that court in 1889, and had been there since, besides being charged at Rotherham and Barnsley on other occasions. Evidence of the offences was given. Wragg was fined 40s. and costs, and Dobson £4/4s/6d., including costs, or two months' imprisonment in default.

---

21 The complainant Michael Ellison owned the shooting rights, rather than the land. However, a Michael Joseph Ellison is listed in 1891 as agent for the Duke of Norfolk [WD].

The above tells us that Dobson was more than just a 'pot-poacher'. In the eyes of the prosecutors, he was a professional. There was another case in the Autumn of 1890 which shows that some local gamekeepers were also becoming exasperated by the thought of an encounter with Ernest Dobson. The *Sheffield Independent* for Friday 24 October reported as follows:

ROTHERHAM BOROUGH POLICE COURT.

Before the ex-Mayor (Ald. Mason), Ald. George Wragg, Mr. J. M. Habershon[22], and Mr. C. J. Stoddart. GAME TRESPASS at Scholes. Oswald Wragg, an old offender, was charged with trespassing in pursuit of game, on land belonging to Earl Fitzwilliam, in the occupation of James Lowe, at Scholes, on Oct. 1st. Mr. Hickmott prosecuted, and said the defendant and a man named Ernest Dobson, an experienced shot, were in a turnip field. Wragg was walking up and down, and a pheasant got up, and Dobson shot and killed it. They ran to the place and endeavoured to find the bird, and Luke Carrington, a keeper, followed them.[23] Seeing Carrington, defendant ran across a stubble field, and, thinking the keeper had gone, began to range Scholes plantation. Carrington went towards him and shouted, "It's no use bothering with you; I know you too well." Dobson had been apprehended on another charge, and he was in prison. The Chief Constable said the defendant had been convicted 26 times. Fined £2 and costs or one month's imprisonment.

1891

We learn from *White's Directory* for 1891 that Ernest Dobson's father Joseph was now living in Hesley Lane, in the part of Thorpe Hesley which was then regarded as being in Chapeltown, and that he was now clerk of the Anglican parish.

---

22 John Matthew Haberson J.P. was a manufacturer in Rotherham, as well as an Alderman, and Mayor in 1871.
23 Luke Carrington of Greasborough, was listed as a gamekeeper in 1891 [WD].

(We can only imagine his attitude towards his only son's repeated appearances in the courts, especially in Golden Jubilee Year).

In March 1891 Dobson was summoned to appear in Rotherham yet again, but once again did not show up. The reports of the proceedings in the *Sheffield Evening Telegraph* on Monday 16 March 1891 and in the *Sheffield Independent* for Tuesday 17 March 1891 also show that the magistrates too were now at a loss as to what to do with Dobson, when he appeared before them.

AN INVETERATE POACHER

This morning before the Rotherham West Riding Police Court, Mr. H. Jubb (in the chair) and Colonel Hoole, Ernest Dobson, John Copley, and Thomas Hoyland were summoned for having committed game trespass on land in the occupation of Mr. Merriman farmer, of Wentworth, on the 2nd inst. According to the evidence of Walter Dickinson the three defendants were seen in Mr. Merriman's field. A hare was put up, and Copley fired at it. Copley and Hoyland were each fined 40s and costs.

Mr. Hickmott, who prosecuted on behalf of Earl Fitzwilliam, stated that Dobson did not appear. Inasmuch the defendant was well known to the Bench, he asked for a warrant. The last time Dobson was before the Court, a lenient view was taken of the case, the man being remanded at large on promising to reform.

Mr. Jubb said he thought Mr. Hickmott was wrong. He (the magistrate) had fined him 40s.

Mr. Hickmott said Dobson had been up since the time referred to by Mr. Jubb. He was remanded at large by Mr. Chambers.

Mr. Jubb: Cannot you employ him as a game keeper? Perhaps there would be required one or two men to look after him. (Laughter.)

But it was not just a laughing matter. There were many others whom the magistrates regarded as 'inveterate poachers'. Another example of the hopelessness of the situation had been reported in the *Sheffield Evening Telegraph* on Monday 5 January 1891.

The Jubilee Poacher

AN INVETERATE POACHER.
PAID SUFFICIENT IN FINES TO BUY A COTTAGE.

At the Rotherham West Riding Police Court today, Enoch Swift, a well-known character belonging to Bradgate, was charged with trespassing in search of game on the Wilcock plantation of Earl Fitzwilliam, on the 2nd December. The case was proved, and the Chairman, addressing the prisoner, remarked that that was the 29th time he had been before that Bench on similar charges, and the penalties and fines inflicted reached an amount which would have enabled him to purchase a cottage.

Prisoner (sadly): Aye, they would.

The Chairman: And the wages the time you lost poaching would have furnished the cottage.

Prisoner: True; I'm very sorry for it, sir.

The Chairman: You are an inveterate poacher, and it's no use talking to you now, I am afraid. You must pay a fine of 40s. and costs, or go to prison for a month.

Sometimes Dobson pursued his activities as far as Doncaster. Reports in the *Sheffield Daily Telegraph* and *Sheffield Independent* on Monday 8 June 1891, tell us that he gave a false address to the court on each occasion.

DONCASTER DIVISION

Ernest Dobson, collier, South Kirkby, charged at the West Riding Court, Doncaster, on Saturday, with game trespass on Mr. Warde-Aldam's estate at Frickley. Defendant has been before the West Riding Magistrates at Rotherham no less than 36 times. He was ordered to pay 40s. or prison for a month, and accepted the alternative.

HIS 37th CONVICTION.

Ernest Dobson, collier, South Kirby, was summoned at Court, Doncaster, on Saturday, for the 37th time, and the charge was of having trespassed in pursuit of game at Clayton. Elijah Hickton, game keeper, Hooton Pagnell, proved the case, saying the defendant was beating his hedges with a stick; he had no gun or dog. Fined 40s. and costs, one month's imprisonment in default.

According to the prison register, Dobson was committed to Wakefield jail by the Sheffield Magistrates on 3 July 1891 for game trespass, and for 14 days, unless he paid a fine; but this time the fine was paid and he was discharged the following day. So far as the prison was concerned this was his 27th conviction, though this was less than the figure cited to the magistrates; but the same source refers to a 28th conviction, in that he was committed to Wakefield on 20 July by the Wakefield Magistrates. They had sentenced him to seven days hard labour, unless he paid a fine of 14s/6d, for being 'drunk and riotous'; but he was in fact released on 25 July. Finally, the Register shows Dobson committed on 28 July by Rotherham magistrates for 28 days unless he paid £3/9s/6d. The prison authorities recorded this as his 29th conviction; but he was released on 22 August. It had been a busy summer for all concerned!

The last of these convictions was noticed by the *Sheffield Independent* on Tuesday 28 July 1891:

ROTHERHAM WEST RIDING POLICE COURT.

Ernest Dobson, labourer, pleaded guilty to game trespass on land occupied by Mr. George Merryman, between Wentworth and Thorpe, on March 2nd last.[24] Prisoner and two men named Hoyland and Copley, who had a gun, were ranging the fields. Dobson started a hare and Copley fired, and because be missed it Dobson swore at him. Dobson farther up the hedge found a keeper watching them.

---

24 George Merrymann is listed as a farmer in the hamlet of Barrow, Wentworth in 1891 [WD]

Hoyland and Copley had already been fined. Mr. Hickmott added that on the last occasion the prisoner was before the court his promised not to offend again, and on the strength of that promise the chairman (Mr. Chambers) remanded him at large. He believed the prisoner was trespassing in pursuit of game the next night. Mr. F. P. Rhodes (clerk to the court) said there were 38 previous convictions: the fines amounted to over £40. Last July prisoner was committed at Wakefield for seven days, and on June 6th at Doncaster for one month, and on January 19th he was convicted at Rotherham. Prisoner was fined 40s. and costs.

We can appreciate the difficulty which the authorities had in keeping track of this man. On the one hand, they could never be sure of the number of his previous offences. On the other, there was the problem of calculating how much he still owed in outstanding fines, and how many days he should spend in jail, for current offences and old ones.

1892

Dobson's offences to date had been committed in what we now call South Yorkshire; but in 1892 he appeared in court in Pontefract. On Monday 6 June the *Sheffield Independent* reported as follows:

PONTEFRACT AND DISTRICT.
POACHING ON THE DARRINGTON ESTATE.
SIXTY-THREE PREVIOUS CONVICTIONS.

At Pontefract on Saturday, Ernest Dobson and Oswald Wragg, notorious poachers, of Featherstone, were charged with poaching at Darrington, on land where game was preserved by Mr. John Shaw. Dobson was seen to shoot a hare and Wragg assisted in wrapping it in a handkerchief. Dobson acknowledged having shot a rabbit, and he told the magistrates that he seldom missed when he put his gun to his shoulder. He had been

63 times previously convicted and Wragg 11 times. Fined £2 each and costs, or one month. John Wilks, John Dutton, and Henry Radley, all of Featherstone, were fined 9s. 2d. each for trespassing on Lord Mashum's [sic] estate at Ackton. [25]

On this occasion, the Pontefract magistrates fined Dobson and specified one month's imprisonment if he did not pay. We know from the Wakefield prison records that he didn't, because he arrived at the prison owing £3/0s/2d in all, and he was not released until 3 July. The magistrates thought that he had 63 previous convictions, but the prison register records 31.

1893

Dobson was convicted three times in 1893, although none of these was reported in local newspapers, and we must rely on the Wakefield prison registers for the facts. The first offence was for 'game trespass', which the Pontefract magistrates, sitting on 3 June, punished with a fine of £2/19s/9d or 1 month's imprisonment. There is no record of Dobson paying the fine, so we must assume that he served his time. The second conviction, on 3 July, was unusual, in that it consisted of damaging a tree, although we saw that he had been convicted of wilfully damaging growing underwood in 1877. On this occasion, the Rotherham magistrates fined Dobson 35 shillings, but again he could not or would not pay and served the full term of imprisonment, which was 28 days. The third conviction was again for game trespass. This time it was the Sheffield magistrates who imposed a fine of £2/2s/8d, with 28 days in default; but again Dobson chose to do the time.

1895

On Monday 16 September 1895 the *Sheffield Evening Telegraph* had occasion to refer to Ernest Dobson once again:

---

25 Darrington is now in the City of Wakefield, West Yorkshire.

THE "JUBILEE POACHER" AGAIN IN TROUBLE

Ernest Dobson, miner, who has well earned the sobriquet of the "Jubilee poacher,'" was brought before the Rotherham West Riding Court to-day charged with game trespass. According to the statements of Mr. Hickmott who appeared to prosecute on behalf of Earl Fitzwilliam, and William Robinson, a woodman, it seemed that Dobson could not resist the temptation for a little sport when favourable opportunity presented itself. On the 4th September Dobson was seen in a field in the parish of Greasborough moving about in the long grass. There were rabbits there. He went to two rabbit holes, pulling them open. When spoken to he said he was looking for mushrooms, although the state of his clothing indicated that he had been in closer contact with the earth than the gathering of this edible necessitated.

Inspector Plowright informed the bench that the prisoner did not usually answer these summonses. There were convictions recorded in the court, but adding on those at Barnsley and Sheffield, the number would come up to 70 at least. Prisoner had been fined 40 shillings and costs, and had also been committed.

Mr Hickmott stated that the last time was before the Court, he promised to reform, and on the strength of this assurance the present chairman (Mr. Chambers), let him off (laughter).

Police Constable Hutchinson remarked that he had been since then.

Mr. Hickmott said he had just been told the keeper had caught him the same week, and Mr. Chambers had let him off. For that offence he was fined. (Laughter). Mr Chambers said the bench had decided to inflict a penalty of 40s. or one month's imprisonment with hard labour.

There was also a report in the *Sheffield Independent* on Tuesday 17 September 1895. From this we learn that at the close of proceedings the Chairman (Mr. Chambers) asked "Does he pay or go to gaol?" Inspector Plowright replied "He generally goes to gaol"; and a fine of 40s and costs or one month's imprisonment was imposed.

1896

The *Sheffield Daily Telegraph* ran the next story on Monday 3 February 1896. This time, Dobson went further afield again, into Derbyshire, where he used an alias, and was involved in a different kind of crime. Although the authorities realised who he was, he seems to have fooled them when it came to the number of his previous convictions for poaching.

BOLSOVER POLICE AFFRAY.

Ernest Dobson, alias Slynn, navvy, was charged at the Chesterfield County Police Court, on Saturday, with assaulting Police Sergeant Clarke and Police Constable Buxton, and also with rescuing a prisoner at Hillstown, Bolsover, on the 20th ult. The prisoner was one of gang of navvies who set on the officers while they were taking to the lock-up a man charged with stealing a coat. Several of the men had already been sent to gaol for six months, and the Bench dealt with him in like manner. The prisoner, who used to be a collier at Thorpe Hesley, had 73 previous convictions recorded against him, five of them being for game trespasses.

Dobson was a classic recidivist. He soon reverted to poaching, and on home territory. On 7 September, he was convicted of game trespass by the Rotherham magistrates, and ordered to pay 56 shillings (£2 16 shillings) or spend 28 days in jail. As usual he did the time, and was released on 4 October. However he then went down to Retford in Nottinghamshire, with almost inevitable consequences. This report appeared in the *Sheffield Independent* on Tuesday 17 November 1896.

GAME TRESPASS AT RETFORD.

Yesterday, at Retford, Charles Mellows, Dobson, and Sutton, were summoned for game trespass on October 31st on land belonging to Mr E.E. Harcourt-Vernon, J.P. Mr. Gough, gamekeeper, stated that about 4.15 p.m. he was in the Lodge Hall plantation, when he saw Dobson in the

The Jubilee Poacher

carriage drive. From his position he was able to see up and down. He waited there for some time and saw someone coming, and then heard a whistling.

After a while another whistle was given, and two of the men called out, "All right, we have got it." He went down into the wood, and witness followed him. Sutton had found a rabbit in some thorns, and Mellows called out, "Look clear, he is here," and threw a large stone at the rabbit.

Witness came out of his hiding place and called out, "Now then, what's the game?" The men bolted, and witness called out, "I know you all; you need not run." Mellows had a dog and witness saw another dog in the cover. When witness served the summons with Sergeant Stringfellow, Dobson said, "I know I am a -------". I told them we should get caught. I went with them." Fined 10s. 6d. each and costs.

We note that this trespass was committed on land belonging to a Justice of the Peace! But in the 19th century many of the magistrates were landowners.

1899

The *Sheffield Daily Telegraph* for Tuesday 21 February 1899 carried a familiar tale of game trespass, though mixed this time with an element of violence. The story also confirms that Dobson had recently been away from the district.

THE JUBILEE POACHER AGAIN FINED

Ernest Hobson, of Thorpe Hesley, now known by the name of the "Jubilee" poacher, was summoned at the Rotherham West Riding Police Court, yesterday, for having trespassed in pursuit of game land over which Earl Fitzwilliam has the right of sporting. At 11.30 o'clock in the morning of the 7th inst., an underkeeper, named Harkiss, found the defendant kneeling by a rabbit hole in a field occupied by Mr. Bowman,

Wentworth.[26] The footpath was a considerable distance away. Defendant ran off but the keeper followed, and overtook him. Defendant then produced a stone, and threatened to dash out the keeper's brains. In his pocket were five or six small stones. Defendant admitted he was an old offender, but said on this occasion he was not guilty. A keeper had struck him with his stick. Superintendent Quest stated that the defendant had been up 41 times previously, chiefly for game trespass. He had not been before the court for several years. Mr Hickmott who prosecuted, understood the defendant had been away from the district. Fined 20s and costs.

The Wakefield prison registers confirm that Dobson was committed to prison in February 1899 and discharged on 19 March. It also tells us that he was now 43 years of age and that this was his 36th conviction (contradicting what the magistrates had been told.)

1900

There is only one conviction recorded this year, in the *Sheffield Daily Telegraph* for Friday 21 September 1900.

CITY AND COUNTY

Ernest Dobson, miner, of Masborough[27] was yesterday fined 10s. and costs for trespassing in pursuit of game on land in the occupation of Joseph Cooper.[28] Defendant had 35 previous convictions recorded against him.

---

26 Sidney Bowman is listed as a farmer in Thorpe Hesley in 1891 [WD].
27 This should have been Masbrough, not Masborough, which is near Sheffield. The former was described in 1862 as 'a populous suburb of Rotherham.' {DD, 1862]
28 In *Church, Chapel & Community*, Melvyn Jones pointed out that the Joseph Cooper living in Scholes in 1833 was head botanic gardener at Wentworth Woodhouse; but that was almost 70 years previous to the relevant conviction. This Joseph Cooper is almost certainly the farmer, born in Scholes in 1854, who was recorded in the Census of 1891, who was now working 'on his own account' there.

1901

There seems to have been only one conviction this year; but the reports of it in the *Sheffield Evening Telegraph* on Wednesday 13 March 1901 and in the *Barnsley Chronicle* on Saturday 16 March 1901 differ in several respects. The first report reads as follows:

A PERSISTENT POACHER

At Barnsley today before Mr. T. Norton and other magistrates, Ernest Dobson, ripper, of Thorpe Hesley was charged with trespassing in search of game on Earl Fitzwilliam's preserves at Westwood, Tankersley on the 29th of January. Mr. J. Carrington defended. At ten o'clock on the 29th January John Wright, gamekeeper, saw the defendant with a dog beating for rabbits, and told him he would be reported. Two days later he was seen digging at a rabbit hole, and he had been on the ground shooting pheasants. Defendant had been times 36 time convicted, and a fine of 20s. and costs was imposed.

The second report was as follows.

CHEEKY

Ernest Dobson, described as a ripper of Thorpe Hesley, was charged with trespassing on land at Wentworth, over which Earl Fitzwilliam has the right of shooting. Mr. J. Carrington who prosecuted, said that on the night of the 29th January, defendant was seen in West Wood by a gamekeeper. He had no stick or gun; but a mongrel dog belonging to him was "working." Defendant was told he would be reported, but since that day had been caught shooting pheasants in the same place. John Wright, gamekeeper, and Edward Winch, head keeper, proved this statement and defendant was fined 20/- and costs. A list of 35 previous convictions was recorded against him, dating from 1875 onwards.

1902

A report in the *Sheffield Daily Telegraph* on Tuesday 28 January 1902 makes us wonder how Ernest Dobson thought he could ever get away with the ridiculous excuses he sometimes gave the court.

EXPENSIVE SPORT AT WORTLEY.

"It's only for a bit of sport in a day time. I've never been a night poacher in my life". This was the answer Ernest Dobson, labourer, of Thorpe Hesley, gave at the Barnsley West Riding Police Court, when charged with having trespassed on land at Wortley, belonging to the Earl of Wharncliffe, on the 14th June last. On the day in question the defendant was seen with another man in a field adjoining the Wharncliffe Chase. Christopher Parkin, a keeper, went towards him, and on his running away chased him to a public house, where he admitted the offence, and also a second alleged to have been committed a month earlier. Summonses were issued, but Dobson had only just been apprehended. A long list of previous convictions was recorded against the defendant, who was fined 40s. and costs.

As far as we know, Dobson's next appearance was in Sheffield. The *Sheffield Daily Telegraph* for Wednesday 24 September 1902 carried a report of the proceedings before the Police Court.

A PRACTISED POACHER.

Ernest Dobson, labourer, of Thorpe Hesley, was summoned for game trespass. On Monday week a gamekeeper saw the defendant on land at Smithy Wood, over which Mr. Percy Hoole and others have the right of shooting.[29] Two dogs were with him, and one was working at a rabbit

---

29 During the Civil War, Rotherham sided with the Parliamentary party, and the loyalist Grammar School Master, Charles Hoole, was compelled to give up his post, and leave the town.

hole. The defendant had been summoned 63 times previously, on nearly every occasion for game trespass. He had appeared at every Court in the Riding. A fine of 30s., or a month's imprisonment, was imposed.

There was also a conviction this year for an entirely different kind of offence, and one which was unique in terms of Ernest Dobson's career, so far as we know. The reports in the *Sheffield Daily Telegraph* for 3 June 1902 and the *Belper News* for 6 June 1902 tell us very little, but were nevertheless sensational in their day.

GENERAL NEWS.

Ernest Dobson, miner, well-known the police, was at Rotherham Monday fined 40s. and costs for indecency at Thorpe Hesley.

The offence was also noted by a Thorpe Hesley man named Aaron Allott who kept a journal.[30]

Ernest Dobson sentenced to a month's imprisonment for indecency against young lads at Thorpe Hesley by Rotherham Magistrates on June 2nd 1902.

Curiously, Allott noted a similar offence, by another Thorpe Hesley miner, only four months later:

John Clark a Pit Sinker at Thorpe Hesley sentenced at Rotherham to 4 months imprisonment for indecent assault on a lad age 8 belonging to Teddy Tilley of the Huts Bottom of Thorpe Hesley on Oct 13th 1902.

The report of this in the *Sheffield Daily Telegraph* for 14 October 1902 tells us no more; but the Magistrates expressed their dismay at the number of indecent assaults recently presented to them, and one of them blamed the general increase

---

30   See my book on Aaron Allott - *Flower Shows, Wild Beasts and Horrible Murders* published on chivalryandwar.co.uk.

in crime on drink, and the growth in the number of clubs, which he hoped that a forthcoming Licensing Act would do something to curb.

1903

1903 was another bumper year for Ernest Dobson. The first of three convictions (or rather series of convictions) for poaching and related offences in February, July and October, was recorded in the Wakefield prison register on 14th January. This tells us that Dobson had appeared before the Pontefract Magistrates for game trespass and was sentenced to one month's imprisonment in default of payment of fines totalling £2/19s/6d. This was recorded as his 43rd conviction; and, as usual, he chose to do the time, being released only on 11th February 1903. In July he was back before the magistrates in Rotherham and was sentenced to a further month, in default of payment of a further 56 shillings. This was recorded in Wakefield as being his 44th conviction, and he was released on 14 August 1903.

The events of October 1893 were more unusual. This time, they were recorded in the newspapers, starting with the *Yorkshire Evening Post* for Monday 5 October 1903, which reported:

ASSAULTING A GAMEKEEPER.

Barnsley, to-day, Ernest Dobson, of Thorpe Hesley, was sent to gaol for one month for assaulting a gamekeeper, and for another month in default of the payment of fines for poaching. This was Dobson's 41st appearance before the magistrates.

Then, on 6 October 1903 the *Sheffield Daily Telegraph* reported as follows:

CONVICTIONS RAPIDLY ACCUMULATING.

Ernest Dobson, labourer, of Thorpe Hesley, was yesterday, at Barnsley, charged with an assault on John Wasteney, gamekeeper, of Grenoside,

The Jubilee Poacher

and also with poaching on the preserves of Mr. Bellhouse at Grenoside[31] and Earl Fitzwilliam at Wharncliffe Chase,[32] on the 24th ult. The facts have already been 'stated in connection with charges against two men, who took part in each of the "events." There were forty previous convictions against Dobson, who was fined 10s. and costs in each poaching case, and committed to goal for a month for the assault.

Finally the *Barnsley Chronicle* Saturday 10 October 1903 carried two stories about what it called 'the Wortley Poaching Case'.

ANOTHER PUNISHED. Harry Clarke, miner, Owlerton, appeared in answer to two charges of game trespass on land at Wortley and also a charge of having assaulted Joseph Wasteney, gamekeeper to Mr. Bellhouse. Defendant pleaded guilty to all the charges. W. Robinson (Messrs. Tyas and Son), who prosecuted, stated that defendant was one of the three men, who, on the 24th August were found trespassing on land at Wortley, in the occupation Mr. Bellhouse, and of which the Earl of Wharncliffe has the right of shooting. The men had with them two snap dogs, which they set to range the field where rabbits were preserved. Wasteney went up to them and asked them what they doing there, and they replied in abusive and most threatening language. The keeper followed them a short distance, and as the men were getting over the fence to go into the Earl of Wharncliffe's field, he told that he would report the matter. This remark annoyed them, and all three returned and struck and kicked Wasteney, knocking him to the ground, causing him great pain. After ranging in the next field for a short time, the keeper (Harold Rylett) spoke to them, and then left. Evidence was given by Joseph and Harold Rylett (gamekeeper to the

---

31 A Mr E.L.W. Bellhouse was managing director of Joseph Ashforth & Co. Ltd in Owler Lane in 1891 The company had a steelworks and manufactured nuts and bolts in Mowbray Street in 1881. [WD].

32 The writer must have meant the Earl of Wharncliffe.

Earl of Wharncliffe).[33] Defendant denied kicking Wasteney but admitted that all three struck him. In each of the cases of game trespass, defendant was fined 5/- and costs, and for the assault, 10/- and costs, or a further 14 days...

THE LAST OF THE WORTLEY POACHING TRIO

Ernest Dobson, labourer, Thorpe Hesley, was summoned on two charges game trespass at Wortley (on land over which the Right Hon. the Earl of Wharncliffe has the rignt of shooting), and also with having assaulted Joseph Westeney, gamekeeper to Mr. Bellhouse, of Stead Springs, Grenoside. Defendant pleaded guilty to all the charges. Mr. W. Robinson, who prosecuted, stated that prisoner was the last to be caught of the three men who were found trespassing land at Wortley, on the 24th August. The facts of the case were precisely similar the evidence given on Wednesday and Friday in last week, when the two others were convicted.

Jos. Wasteney gave evidence, and made out that Dobson was the worst of the three, and assaulted him in the most brutal manner. Harold Rylett (gamekeeper to the Earl of Wharncliffe) also spoke of the trespass on his lordship's estate. Witness was watching from the disused quarry in Wharncliffe Chase, and saw two snap-dogs, belonging to the three men implicated, ranging Warren Wood, but he intercepted them before they were actually amongst the preserves. Asked if he had anything to say, defendant said, "I am the same as the other men. I expect you will make all three alike." (Laughter). The Chairman stated that there were 40 convictions against defendant for all sorts of offences. In each the cases of game trespass he would have to pay fine 10/- and costs, or 14 days: and for the assault, he would have to go prison for a further month.

---

33 According to the Census of 1901, Harold Rylett was a gamekeeper, aged 29 born in Birmingham, who lived in Burncross, Ecclesfield with his wife (aged 37), a son aged 2 and a stepson aged 12: ancestry.co.uk.

It is little wonder that the authorities in Wakefield were a little confused, when Ernest Dobson was finally admitted to the prison that October. They recorded that he had been committed by Barnsley magistrates for assault and game trespass, having been sentenced to two months, 14 days and 14 days in default of payment of various fines; and later recorded his date of release as 2 December 1903, indicating that he had served two months in prison in all; but whether this corresponded precisely with what the court had sentenced him to, and whether or not he paid any of the fines remains unclear.

1904

The Sheffield Daily Telegraph for Friday 29 January 1904 reported as follows:

> A fine of 20s. and costs was yesterday imposed on a Rotherham man, an aged Thorpe Hesley miner named Ernest Dobson, for poaching. It was stated that defendant had been before the Court 24 times for game offences, and had sixteen times been fined 40s. and costs for game trespass. His appearances in all numbered 38, and included wilful damage, drunkenness, and police assault, in addition to the game offences.

We have noted before that Dobson was now, from a modern point of view, only middle-aged, though he was described here as being 'aged'. The other remarkable thing, though is that the magistrates were still confused, or in the dark, about the true extent of his previous offending.

1905

Long before 1905, Ernest Dobson's excuses were wearing thin. What he told the court when he appeared before the Barnsley magistrates that year must surely have been taken with a pinch of salt. The proceedings were reported in the *Barnsley Chronicle* and the *Sheffield Daily Telegraph* for Tuesday 2 May.

> The last of three poachers who were surprised at work on the Wharncliffe Chase at Wortley, on the 30th March, was yesterday brought up on

warrant before Messrs. W. Brady and W. Batty, at Barnsley. His name is Ernest Dobson, labourer, of Thorpe Hesley, and he admitted the offence, though he explained that he had not been so bad, as he got no rabbits, "and I don't reckon to miss 'em when I go," he added. Asked to explain his previous history, which included 46 convictions, of which 32 were for poaching, Dobson observed that it was "all what you call pot-poaching. It isn't very bad." He was fined 40 shillings and costs.

There is confirmation of this in the Wakefield prison register, which tells us that Dobson was committed by Barnsley Magistrates for 1 month for game trespass, in default of payment of fines outstanding, and that he was only discharged on 31 May 1905.

1906

Ernest Dobson appears in the records for the last time in 1906. According to the Wakefield prison register a man called Ernest John Dobson was committed by the Sheffield City Magistrates on 22 January for an attempt to steal brass. This is very different from our Ernest's usual 'line of business', and the use of the middle name John is also puzzling, since the Census of 1861 referred to him as Ernest A. Dobson, and the entry in the parish register relating to his birth states that he was named Ernest Augustus originally. We may even wonder whether this was the same man; but when the prison register notes that he was from Scholes, was 5 feet 10¼ inches tall, with brown hair and an Anglican, and especially that he had 49 previous convictions, we can surely have little doubt.[34]

At the same time, there are puzzling entries which indicate that the prisoner was 52, when we now know that he was only 50; and that he was discharged from prison on the same day as he went in; but all is made clear when we read the relevant reports in the *Sheffield Evening Telegraph* for Wednesday 25 April and in the *Sheffield Daily Telegraph* for Thursday 26 April 1906.

---

34 The same record shows a '1' next to the column 'Education', indicating that previous references to 'Inf.' must refer to 'infants', that is primary education only. (Census information derived from ancestry.co.uk.)

SHEFFIELD CITY SESSIONS.
"TOO VAGUE FOR ANYTHING."

According to the calendar, the charge against Arthur Thorpe (29), collier, Walter Tingle (52), labourer, and Ernest John Dobson (52), labourer, was of attempting to steal engine brasses, the property of T. W. Ward (Ltd.). Soon after Mr. Bramley had opened the case for the prosecution, the Assistant Recorder pointed out that indictment was "too vague for anything." It said no more than that the men were charged with stealing goods and chattels. Mr. Bramley said the prisoners learned at the police court which specific articles they were accused of stealing. By direction of the Assistant Recorder the jury forthwith found the men not guilty.

This explains why Dobson was admitted to and discharged from prison on the same day. He must have been arrested following his appearance before the magistrates and held in custody, pending trial; but then there was no trial at all because, almost as soon as the court was seized of the matter, the Judge decided that was no case to put before the jury.

Some months later, the Wakefield prison register reveals that Ernest John Dobson was committed to Wakefield by the Leeds and by the Pontefract Magistrates, on 22 August and 23 August respectively, for game trespass and [breach of?] a muzzling order, and for using obscene language. The sentence handed down in Leeds was two months in default of payment of £5/12 shillings, whle the Pontefract bench sentenced him to 14 days, in default of payment of 21s/9d. The particulars recorded in Wakefield tell us that this is once again the same Ernest Dobson who was so well known to the courts and the prison (though they got his age and level of education wrong);[35] and (for the umpteenth time) they were all at sea when it came to the number of his previous convictions. We are told with clarity, however, that he was released on 5 September 1906.

And that is the last we hear of him.

---

35 His level of education is recorded this time as '2.'

Two

The Village

The Place

Thorpe Hesley is a village in South Yorkshire (formerly in the West Riding) which is equidistant from Rotherham, Sheffield and Barnsley though, for local government purposes, it is mostly in Rotherham. It sits in rural surroundings, and you can walk or cycle through the fields and woods, to Wentworth Park (about a mile away), or to Wortley Park and Wharncliffe Chase (at a distance of about six miles). The topography was the same in Ernest Dobson's day; but the village was more industrialised then, and it was close to two settlements - Thorncliffe and Elsecar - which were the beating hearts of industrial complexes [see illustrations 5, 6, 8 & 9]. In those days, the Parks and the Chase stood in complete contrast: they were places where one could find peace and quiet, as well as game. Ironically, the contrast is less sharp now, because of de-industrialisation.[36]

As early as 1831 the historian Joseph Hunter described Thorpe Hesley as 'a populous village inhabited for the most part by nailers and agriculturists', while White's Directory of 1838 tells us that the village was 'noted' for the

---

36 The pits in Thorpe Hesley closed in the 1970s. Newton Chambers was taken over in 1971 and subsequently broken up. In 1986 the Department of the Environment listed most of the buildings at what is now the Elsecar Heritage Centre to be of special architectural or historic interest.

manufacture of nails. Communications were relatively good. The industrial villages of Chapeltown, Ecclesfield and Elsecar were all within easy walking distance, while Earl Fitwilliam's estate village of Wentworth was just across the fields, and up the hill. It was not difficult for the traveller to get to Manchester or York by horse or by coach. Thorpe Common was on an ancient route linking Rotherham with Cheshire, through Kimberworth, Chapeltown, Wortley and Green Moor, which had been turnpiked in 1741; and it was only four miles by the turnpike from Thorpe to Rotherham and a further 12 miles to Doncaster, which was on the Great North Road. However, in the mid-19th century tolls were seen as a bar to progress and the toll bars were taken down, though the tollhouses were often left in place. Then, within a few years, the railways arrived.

Poaching had long been endemic in South Yorkshire. The Wortley family (later Earls of Wharncliffe) obtained a grant of free warren with which to create a hunting chase on Wharncliffe Crags in 1252 and built a hunting lodge there in 1510. Hugh de Elland obtained a similar grant in relation to Tankersley Park in the early 14th century. In the 17th century there were deer parks nearby, on Wharncliffe Chase and at Tankersely, Wentworth, and Kimberworth. There were 140 deer in Sir Thomas Wentworth's park at Wentworth in 1633, and 280 in the park at Tankersley in 1653, although these were transferred to Wentworth when Tankersley was given over to ironstone mining in the late 18th century. In 1662, two men from the village were convicted of poaching deer in the 2nd Earl of Strafford's deer-park at Tankersley.[37]

> Thomas Burdet late of Thorpe Hesley in the county of York, yeoman, and Alexander Hill late of the same place, and Taylor, between 10 hours and 11 hours in the night of the same day, the park of the right Honourable William Earl of Strafforth called Tankersley Parke at Tankersley aforesaid in the West Riding of the said county, being fenced off, enclosed and used and protected for the nurturing, conservation and preservation of deer, by force of arms, namely with staffs, swords, and sharpened

---

[37] West Yorkshire Archive Service, Wakefield, turnpikes (deposited plans and annual accounts); Hey,(1979) 80-2; 115-117; Hey (1986), 82; Indictment Book of the West Riding Quarter Sessions, WYAS, Wakefield.

instruments unjustly and illegally broke and entered and the deer in the same park being did then and there with dogs called Grehounds (sic) unjustly and illegally hunt, put to flight and chase And four deer - 2 brace of deer - with the said greyhounds did then and there unjustly and illegally take, kill and carry away against the will and pleasure of the said William Earl of Strafforth without any legitimate entitlement or authority

In 1865, there were was a 'frightful gun accident', which attracted national attention. The following article appeared in the *Morning Advertiser* on Saturday 5 August 1865 and in the *Taunton Courier, and Western Advertiser* on Wednesday 9 August 1865.

An appalling gun accident has occurred at Thorpe Hesley, near Sheffield. The victim was James Myers, aged 49 wood steward to the Duke of Norfolk. On Saturday the deceased took out his gun for the purpose of shooting a couple of rabbits for a Sheffield friend. In getting over a hedge or wall the piece fell from his hands and exploded, lodging its contents in the unfortunate man's head. Shocking to relate, almost one half of the unfortunate man's face was blown away. The charge had entered under the right jaw, and, taking an oblique upward direction, passed out the left side of the face under the eye, laying the inside of the mouth bare, and showing that the roof had been fearfully mutilated. Notwithstanding the appalling nature of his wounds, the deceased managed to walk back, a distance of 160 yards, towards his own garden wall. He stood there for a few seconds and was seen by his son, a young man, 21 years of age, against the wall.

Hunting and poaching have long been part of the Englishman's way of life. So have ale and beer. Whereas Wentworth has only ever had two pubs (*The Rockingham Arms* and the *George & Dragon*), there were three pubs and four beerhouses in Scholes in 1862,[38] and 10 pubs and beerhouses in Thorpe Hesley

---

38 The pubs were the *Effingham Arms*, the *Old Gate*, and the *Bay Horse*.

in 1891, including *The Gate, The Red Lion, The Mason's Arms, The Horse and Tiger, The Golden Ball*39 and *The Travellers* [see illustrations 11, 12 &13]. This can be contrasted with one in Scholes and four in Thorpe now, though the population has increased five-fold in the last century.[40] However, the Northamptonshire poacher James Harker took a very dim view of pubs. He thought they led many a man astray, when he could have been indulging himself in the healthy pleasures of poaching. He also thought that a man who drank habitually would not be fit enough to outrun the gamekeepers. He wrote this in his journal about two of his friends

> My two Pals Spent there [sic] money in Drink. They are both Dead now [1904] through that. One Died in a Lunatic Asylum. Many a time I Have Begged of them to Let the Drink alone and come and roam the Beautiful Fields with me. Sometimes in the Small Hours of the morning when coming Home with a Hare or Pheasant I have peept into a Pub and seen these two sitting fast asleep. Drink Pubs did not Close in those Days [1866] as they do now.

Unlike Wentworth and Wortley, Thorpe Hesley was not an 'estate village' Earl Fitzwilliam may have owned much of the land, but he was not lord of the manor. This bred a certain dissenting tradition, in more senses than one. One result was that Thorpe became a place where Methodism flourished, decades before it acquired its own Anglican parish; and by 1900 there were three chapels in the village, in addition to the parish church [see illustrations 15 & 16].

Another result of relative isolation from the seats of power may have been that there were more poachers than gamekeepers in Thorpe Hesley; but it must be said that there was at least one keeper, Amos Brownhill, who lived here in 1862. He was employed by the Earl of Effingham and then by Earl Fitzwilliam, and on one occasion, ran up against the notorious Joseph 'Beardshall'. The *Sheffield Independent* reported on 29 May 1866:

---

39 Now known as The Ball [see illustration 13].
40 As I write the Mason's Arms has closed. Thorpe Hesley nowadays (2018) has very few shops, though there were clearly many in former times.

Joseph Beardshall, a character well known to the police, appeared in answer to a summons charging him with trespassing in pursuit of game on land at Kimberworth. It seemed that Amos Brownhill, gamekeeper, observed the defendant on the day in question in a field between Hill top and Blackburn, and saw him shoot a hare. On being interrogated and requested to give up the hare, defendant denied that he had one. The gamekeeper seized the defendant, whereupon the latter took up a cinder and threatened to "knock his brains out." [41]

THE PEOPLE

According to Melvyn Jones's excellent *South Yorkshire Mining Villages* (2017)

> The Census of 1841 showed that the population of Thorpe Hesley was 1,239 and Scholes had a population of 315. Of the 446 males living in Thorpe Hesley for whom occupations were given, 82 (18 per cent) were engaged in farming, 130 (29 per cent) in nailmaking and 202 (45 per cent) in mining. Of the 78 males living in Scholes for whom occupations were given in 1841, 17 (22 per cent) were in farming, 11 (14 per cent) were nailmakers and 31 (40 per cent) were miners. And in some Thorpe families in 1841 there were both ironstone and coal miners.

Important changes which took place during Ernest Dobson's childhood and youth and by the time he acquired the nickname of Jubilee Poacher, coalmining had completely eclipsed ironstone mining as the major source of income for the people of Thorpe Hesley and Scholes. Melvyn Jones again:

> Ironstone mining was no longer taking place after 1880 but small collieries were dotted about the area. In 1881 in Scholes out of an adult male population of 102, no fewer than 88 were coalminers. The 1901 25-inch Ordnance Survey map shows Scholes Old Colliery on Little Lane halfway between Scholes and Thorpe, where two small slag heaps still survive, and Scholes Colliery behind Upper Wortley Road on

---

41 DD; *Sheffield Daily Telegraph* and *Independent*, 1864-7.

Thorpe Common. These two collieries belonged to the Mangham family [see illustration 8].

In the late 19th century deeper and deeper shafts were sunk.

> The further expansion of Thorpe Hesley as a mining community dates from the sinking of four collieries by Newton Chambers that were linked to each other in various ways. These were Norfolk Colliery, Smithy Wood Colliery, Barley Hall Colliery [see illustration 17] and Thorpe Colliery [illustration 18]. Barley Hall and Thorpe collieries were exceptional in that they were not connected to a railway and coal was never wound to the surface there. They were ventilation shafts, service shafts and water pumping shafts for Norfolk, Smithy Wood (sunk in 1890) and Thorncliffe (sunk in 1859) collieries.[42]

This reference to the collieries at Thorncliffe reminds us that not all the land around Thorpe Hesley and Scholes belonged to aristocrats. Some of it belonged to Newton Chambers, a firm with a history which began in 1793 when George Newton and Thomas Chambers took a lease to extract coal and ironstone in the Thorncliffe valley near Chapeltown from Earl Fitzwilliam. The company then built the Thorncliffe Ironworks, beside the Blackburn Brook. By the end of the 19th century Newton Chambers was not only mining coal and ironstone: it was operating blast furnaces, coke ovens and chemical plant, and manufacturing stove grates, kitchen ranges and fenders. During the 1890s, it developed its famous Izal disinfectant, which was made from distilled coal tar. In the 20th century, it had a reputation for apprenticeships which were as good as those at Rolls-Royce and manufactured over 1,000 Churchill tanks during the Second World War. It was only taken over in 1971.

Nailmaking also had a long history in Thorpe. Melvyn Jones has also written[43]:

---

42   Thorpe Colliery closed in 1972, Smithy Wood closed in the same year and Barley Hall in 1975.
43   Melvyn Jones in *The People of Thorpe & Scholes*, in *Church, Chapel & Community*, Stephen Cooper, Robert Chesman and Melvyn Jones (privately printed.

The nailmaking industry in 1841 was a domestic one, and the two villages [Thorpe and Scholes] formed part of a long-established nailaking district stretching into Hoyand and South-West into Ecclesfield.... There were two sorts of nailmakers in the new parish [of Thorpe] – nail-factors or manufacturers, and domestic nailmakers.

There were still two nail manufacturers and one nailmaker in Scholes in 1862;[44] but they had largely disappeared from Thorpe Hesley by the 1880s, and the farm labourers now had to cope with a new kind of agricultural depression, brought about by free trade, the advent of steamships and refrigeration, and competition with the U.S.A. and the British colonies.

The occupations of women in 1841 are give in only 46 cases; and, since the local mine owners did not employ women or girls, and there was no local factory-based textile industry, most of these were employed as household servants, especially at Wentworth Woodhouse, but also on local farms.[45] This explains why it was unusual for them to be caught poaching. Being at home so much, they were much less likely to get involved.

The Rich

The inhabitants of Thorpe Hesley were, to an even greater extent than now, surrounded by fields, woods and parkland – notably, Hesley Park Wood, Smithy Wood, Scholes Coppice, Gallery Bottom, Walkworth Wood and Barber Wood, and the deer park attached to Wentworth House. Most of the land belonged to the Earls Fitzwilliam and Effingham, or the Duke of Norfolk. Fitzwilliam was lord of the Manor of Wentworth, Greasborough, Swinton and Tinsley, but also owned much of the land in Thorpe Hesley. Effingham was lord of the manors of Rotherham and Kimberworth, while the Duke owned land around Hesley Wood. In addition Effingham had his principal residence at Thundercliffe Grange, between Rotherham and Ecclesfield.[46] Hesley Hall, on the other hand,

---

44 DD.
45 Jones, op.cit., pp 26-8.
46 The 3rd Earl built Thundercliffe Grange in 1777, when he moved from The Holmes in Rotherham itself. By 1891 it was a private lunatic asylum for 'ladies'. It can now be seen from the M1 motorway near junction 34 (Meadowhall).

was in the possession of a tenant farmer.[47] The Earl of Wharncliffe's mansion and estate village and park at Wortley were only six miles away, while his property at Wharncliffe Chase was even closer.

Earl Fitzwilliam, sometime Lord-Lieutenant of the West Riding of Yorkshire, was the most important local landowner, with the largest house, largest household and most influence in the local area. His mansion, 'Wentworth Woodhouse' dwarfed those of other local dignitaries and was one of the largest in England, with a frontage measuring 600 feet. The Wentworth estate as a whole comprised some 14,000 acres; and this was by no means his only estate. He had 3,000 acres at Malton in the North Riding, he owned the borough of Higham Ferrers in Northamptonshire, and there was the small matter of 66,000 acres in County Wicklow in Ireland. His income from agricultural land, woods, mines, and quarries was considerable; but then there was the coal: output on the Earl's estates increased tenfold between 1799 and 1823, from about 12,500 tons to some 122,000 tons. Fitzwilliam himself calculated in 1827 that the total income from all his estates was £115,000![48] This made him one of the richest men in England; and, unlike some of the other local landlords, he spent much of his time in Yorkshire, though he also had a town house in London's Grosvenor Square.

Wentworth Park was as impressive as Wentworth Woodhouse, or Wentworth House (as it was always known to the family).[49] It was 'well-wooded' and took in over 1,500 acres, was over nine miles in circumference and, although the Park was protected by a stone wall with gatehouses, it was impossible to deny access to the determined trespasser. In 1787 Earl Fitzwilliam had declared himself in favour of vigorous action to protect his property and 'deter the Neighbourhood from coming into the gardens'. This was a Canute-like endeavour: in 1810, one of the Earl's own employees, Smithson the blacksmith at Lawwood colliery, was committed to the Wakefield House of Correction for stealing wheat and flour stored in Wentworth Park, and he must have been only one of many who breached its defences.[50]

---

47 WD 1891.
48 Smith pp 28-33
49 Wentworth Woodhouse became a teacher training college in 1949. It was acquired by a preservation trust in 2016, after some 20 years in private hands.
50 Mee, 162

Stephen Cooper

Wentworth itself was described by *White's Directory* in 1891 as 'a township and large village'. It included part of Thorpe Hesley, and the hamlets of Ashes, Ashcroft, Spital Houses, Barrowfield, Barley Hole [sic], Harley and Hood Hill, the last of these being on the Sheffield and Barnsley turnpike. It had 1,792 inhabitants in 1881 and comprised 2,297 acres of land and 31 acres of water (doubtless on account of the large lakes in Wentworth Park). Poignantly, the Directory reminds us that 'Earl Fitzwilliam is lord of the manor and owner of the soil'; and that he had recently built the new church, at a cost of £25,000 pounds, as well as endowing a Girls' National and Infants' School, a Mechanics' Institute and Reading Room and Library with 200 volumes. The landlord of The Rockingham Arms was Thomas Abson, the village doctor was Dr Horace Carlos Barr, 'surgeon, medical officer of health and 'public vaccinator',[51] the postmistress was Miss Sevilla Armanda Dobson (no relation, one assumes); and the agent for Earl Fitzwilliam was George Ponsonby Talbot, esq., who lived at Cortworth House, which remains the estate office to this day.[52]

Earl Fitzwilliam was a major employer and Wentworth was the headquarters of his farming enterprises, just as Elsecar was the hub of his aristocratic industrial empire. In 1822 the workforce which was served with beef and sixpence each, at the St Thomas's Day feast, included over 240 colliers, employed at six different pits in and around Wentworth and Elsecar; but also 51 husbandry labourers and 39 garden labourers,[53] excluding indoor staff. In the 6th Earl Fitzwilliam's time (1857-1902), there were 84 servants at 'the Big House;' and probably 60 out-door and non-domestic staff. The Earl also employed many hundreds of colliers in his pits at Parkgate (Rotherham), Brampton Bierlow, Elsecar and elsewhere. In 1891, White's listed 19 of his employees in Wentworth:

---

51 Dr Barr owned one of the first cars in Wentworth (photo in the *George & Dragon* pub, July 2017). According to Roy Young, author of *Big House, Little Village*, he later attended some of the miners who went with the 7th Earl to Cocos Island in 1904 in search of buried treasure, and returned with mysterious injuries (see *Earl Fitzwilliam's Treasure Island*, 2016).

52 According to ancestry.co.uk he was born in 1853 in Cape Colony, married Blanche Douglas in Hanover Square in Jubilee Year 1887, had two children, was still Fitzwilliam's agent in 1911 and died at Worksop in 1924.

53 WWM A 1543, cited by Melvyn Jones in the *Hallamshire Historian*, volume 1, no 1 (*The St Thomas's Day Charity Donation*).

Frank Bartlett, huntsman
Frederick Beck, second whip
Thomas Bonson, first whip
Mrs Cecilia Cape, housekeeper
Dick Joseph, head woodman
William Dickie, clerk of the works
William Foster, gas engineer
H.B. Hans Hamilton, private secretary to Earl Fitzwilliam (Hoober House)
Frederick Inglis, park keeper
William McKie, head gamekeeper
Arthur Paterson, farm bailiff
Mrs Eliza Reeves, dairymaid
James Robinson, stud groom
Frederick Romain, house steward
Joseph Showler, saddler
George Octagon Smith, lodgekeeper[54]
John Smith, head groom
Frederick Thirlby, head gardener
John Thomas Woodward, plumber

We also know, from the Household Accounts preserved in the Wentworth Woodhouse Muniments, that the Earl incurred regular expenditure on the employment of gamekeepers, park-keepers and lawyers, in order to police his estate.[55] Ernest Dobson must surely have crossed swords with several of these men, and on many occasions.

In the early 19th century, the Earls Fitzwilliam were Whigs, meaning that they were in favour of parliamentary reform in 1832, but not that they were in favour of any radical re-structuring of society. They were philanthropists who treated their colliery employees well and did their best to relieve and educate

---

54 Octagon Lodge lies between Wentworth village and the stable block at Wentworth Woodhouse. Presumably the eponymous lodge keeper was born there and named after it.

55 See for example 1857: £507 on park keeping, £411 on game keeping, compared with £312 on hunting and £2,961 on housekeeping: SCL, WWM A-176.

the poor, for example providing their employees with a Mechanic's Institute in Wentworth, and their children with schools.[56] They were even prepared to allow the Chartists to hold meetings on their land (just as their 18th century predecessors had been willing to allow the Methodists to preach on their estates); but there is no reason to believe that they were critics of the game laws, which underpinned their enjoyment of their estates. Later in the century, they built the village of Bradfield, at the heart of their grouse moors in Derbyshire, where the largest landowners (apart from themselves) were Francis Sutton esq., R.H.R. Wilson esq., the Earl of Wharncliffe, the Duke of Norfolk, Messrs Thomas Wragg junior and W. Wing. It should also be mentioned that the Earls were great builders, and the patrons of many churches, schools, mechanics' institutes, hospitals, and enterprises of all kinds. In 1891, the 6th Earl sat on the board of the Sheffield Savings Bank, alongside the Duke of Norfolk, the Earl of Wharncliffe, and two other members of the latter's family.

THE POOR

Life in Thorpe Hesley must have been 'nasty, brutish and short' for some. Coalmining was the most dangerous of the three main occupations available to men. There is a reference to a fatality in 1817 in the *Old Ecclesfield Diary*: "George Hartley and son of Thorp Suffocated and Starved to Death Opening and Cleaning and Old Water Gate at the Coal Pitts in Hesley Park Novr." There is also a large number of informative accounts of mining accidents in local newspapers. For example this from 1847:

> On Wednesday 19 August 1847 Thomas Burgin, who was a 40 year old banksman at the Haggs Pit, between Thorpe and Chapeltown, fell down the shaft. An inquest was held the following day before T. Badger, Esq., Coroner, at Thos. Sayles's, the Blacksmiths' Arms in Thorpe Hesley. It appeared that, at about seven o'clock on the morning in question, the deceased had drawn up an empty 'corve' in which he had been lowering some men into the pit, and had then thrown the landing band across the

---

56 See *Employer, Employee Relationships*, Graham Mee, in *Essays in the Economic & Social History of South Yorkshire*, ed. Sidney Pollard & Colin Holmes (S.Y.C.C., 1976); and Mee, 20-1.

pit mouth, which is used for running the corves from over the pit shaft to the embankment; but he did not take the precaution of seeing that it was fastened by a spring, and stepped onto the board for the purpose of doing something to the chain which secured the corve. The table on which the corve rested tipped over, and he was thrown to the bottom, about 88 yards below. The Jury returned a verdict of Accidental Death.[57]

There was another inquest in September 1856, this time at the Red Lion Inn in Thorpe, but again presided over by the Coroner Badger, regarding Samuel Smith, aged 20, and Samuel Hodgson, aged 14, who had been killed the previous day by an explosion of fire-damp, at the Grange Lane Colliery, which belonged to Joseph Stenton of Ecclesfield. The pit had been sunk only recently, and the workings, which were not extensive, were not yet complete. Two other men, named Fox and Willoughby Wood, were seriously injured. Thirty years later, we read of another fatality nearby.[58]

THE FATAL ACCIDENT AT SCHOLES COLLIERY. INQUEST THIS DAY. This morning inquest was held at the Blacksmiths Arms, Thorpe Hesley, before the Coroner, Mr. D. Wightman, upon the bodies of Arthur Smith, aged 15, and Julius Aithur Smith, who were employed at the Scholes Colliery, and who were killed by a fall of coal Friday last. Mr. Wardell, one of Her Majesty's inspectors of mines, was present at the inquiry, as was also Messrs. G. Mangham and Jenkinson.

Joseph Allott., a miner employed at the pit, and Charles Hall, steward, were called, and asserted that the fall of roofing had arisen through a slip in the coal which had broken down a portion of the propping. Allott, who was working about two hundred yards from the place where the coal fell when the accident happened, assisted getting the deceased out. He afterwards examined the spot and found that there had been

---

57 *Sheffield Independent*, Saturday 21 August 1847.
58 *Sheffield Independent*, Saturday 27 September 1856; *Sheffield Evening Telegraph*, 22 June 1887 and *Sheffield Independent*, 23 June, 1887.

some wood "set" and the fall had come over it. There were many slips, he said, in the pit, and this particular one was visible after the deceased had "bared" it, but not before. He thought the accident happened in spite of any care or precaution that might have been taken. It was with some difficulty that the unfortunate men were extricated, and Arthur Smith was found to be dead. Julius Smith, too, was so badly crushed that there was really no hope of his recovery. He was removed to Rotherham Infirmary, and died there the following day. Inspector Wardall expressed himself as being satisfied that the deaths were the result of an accident, a verdict of "Accidental death" in both cases was returned.

Working hours were long, holidays were few and the working man's life was controlled by the criminal rather than the civil law. There is a good example of this, reported in the *Sheffield Daily Telegraph* for Tuesday 31 July 1866.

> Samuel Sanderson, miner, of Thorpe Hesley, was brought up a charge of unlawfully neglecting his work at the Grange Colliery, near Kimberworth. Mr. Whitfield appeared to prosecute on behalf of Messrs. Chambers and Son, and stated that the defendant was charged with absenting himself from his employment without giving the proper notice. The rules of the colliery provided 28 days' notice of intention to leave. There were, however, some aggravated circumstances connected with this case. At the time he left his employment the defendant was indebted to his masters to the extent of 30 shillings, which had been advanced to him. On the very day he left it appeared that he drew from his masters £5 or £6, a good deal of which was due to under-hands whom he went away without paying. He never gave notice of his intention to leave. Messrs. Chambers and Son therefore felt it their duty to press the charge against him, and it might also be mentioned that it was the desire of the defendant's fellow-workmen that example should be made of the man who had behaved himself so ill to his masters. Mr. Mark Davy, the manager, gave evidence in accordance with this statement. The defendant was able to earn 5 or 6 shillings per day. He left on the 16th of

June, and had since been at Barnsley. The Bench evidently considered this an aggravated case, and ordered the defendant to be committed to the House of Correction for one month.

There is another example of harsh working conditions twenty years later, reported in the *Sheffield Evening Telegraph* for Wednesday 8 June 1887:

A Thorpe Hesley Miner Heavily Fined. Frank Smith, a miner at the Parkgate Drift Pit of Messrs. Newton, Chambers, and Co., was charged with infringing the rules at the pit by neglecting to sprag every two yards of the coal worked by him. A deputy named Alfred Wroe stated that when he made his visit to the defendant's working place on the day named he found it in a dangerous condition, and ordered them to build up two packs. Defendant had been the company's service 16 years without complaint. For the defence, a miner named George Smith, stated that the farthest props were taken out in order that the roof might fall. Charles Booker gave similar evidence, and added that it was the usual practice to remove the props order that the roof might come down. Defendant was fined 30s. and costs.

Conditions in the home were also primitive, by modern standards. Families were more numerous, but infant mortality was very high and health care was poor. In addition, there was an inadequate supply of clean water. In 1849, a local doctor felt moved to write this blistering letter to the editor of the *Sheffield Independent*.[59]

To THE EDITOR —

Will you permit me, through the medium of your journal, to call the attention of the authorities to the truly filthy and unhealthy condition in which the village of Thorpe Hesley now is? More than one half of the cottages are in an unfit state to be inhabited, owing to the sulphuretted

---

59 *Sheffield Independent*, Saturday 29 September 1849.

hydrogen generated from the accumulation of refuse matter by which the dwellings are surrounded. As medical officer of the district, I have already had one case of Asiatic cholera in this village during the past week, independent of the many cases of diarrhoea and dysentery which have come under my notice; and feel certain that, unless some immediate steps are taken, either cholera or fever of a typhoid character will, ere long, rage in this nursery of disease.

ERASMUS STONE, Surgeon.
Masbro' Bridge, Rotherham, Sept. 27, 1849.

There was even a case, almost forty years later, when some local people resorted to stealing water.[60]

Betsy Gillott, Ann Casson and Sarah Ann Butcher of Thorpe Hesley were each summoned for stealing water, the property of the Rotherham Corporation, on the 9th February. Mr. S. Brown, Town Clerk, prosecuted and said the defendants were liable to a penalty not exceeding £5 each. Police Constable Adams proved that Gillott fetched two buckets of water from a house occupied by Sarah Armitage, which was within the limits of the borough of Rotherham. The other two defendants also got water from places where taps belonging the Corporation were fixed. Casson and Butcher denied the offence. The summonses were dismissed, but the Bench pointed out that if the defendants came before the Court again they would not be so leniently dealt with.

Given these conditions, at work and at home, affecting both men and women, it is not surprising that some of the people of Thorpe Hesley and Scholes – and especially the men and the boys – looked to the countryside to supplement their diet, and provide them with sport, nor that they sometimes decided to flout the law, when it stood in their way.

---

60 *Sheffield Daily Telegraph*, Friday 11 March 1887.

The Church

In the 19th century, it was certainly criminal to take game on private land; but what was to stop people from helping themselves? In theory the Church, in its various forms, was a powerful force, which preached that it was wrong to engage in poaching. Both the 8th commandment (which prohibited theft) and the 10th (which prohibited covetousness) said so. Moreover, the Church's power was increasing in the 19th century. The land for the parish church in Thorpe Hesley was donated by Earl Fitzwilliam in 1836, building work took place between 1837 and 1839 (and was largely paid for by Fitzwilliam and the Earl of Effingham) and the ceremony of consecration took place on Whit Tuesday, 1840, when the Countess of Effingham provided 'a cold collation.'[61]

No less than three Methodist chapels were built in the village in the early years of Queen Victoria's reign, and one of these was re-built in Edward VII's time [see illustration 15 & 16]. Whereas *White's Directory* had listed only one chapel in the village in 1837, the same publication noted in 1862 that "the Wesleyan, Primitive and Reform Methodists have each chapels here" while in 1891 it noted that the dates when these erected were 1797, 1859 ad 1856, but referred to the Reform Methodists as the United Free Methodists. What is less well known is that an Orange Lodge was opened in 1862 at the Victoria Inn, when 30 candidates were initiated, and it was recorded that:

> At the conclusion of the proceedings, the brethren partook of an excellent dinner, served in the good old Yorkshire style, after which the usual loyal and Protestant toasts were gone through, and the brethren separated highly satisfied with the day's proceedings. This is the third lodge that has been opened within eighteen months, within a mile or two of each other.[62]

The Victorians certainly believed that a religious upbringing would bring an improvement in the morality of the working classes; and that the foundation of other institutions would work towards the same end. In May 1888, Lady Alice

---

61 *Sheffield and Rotherham Independent*, cited in *Church Chapel & Community*..
62 *Barnsley Chronicle*, Saturday 15 March 1862.

Fitzwilliain laid the foundation stone of a mechanics' institute at Thorpe Hesley [see illustration 14], and this was opened on 1 October, by Sir F.T.Mappin M.P. who made a lengthy speech, essentially expressing the hope that the new Institute would be

> A centre of harmony where every man in the neighbourhood, irrespective of party feeling or religious difference might come and associate with his neighbour; where, in addition to amusement and instruction, brotherly and neighbourly feeling would be promoted...[and where] working men [could] meet together and derive instruction and amusement without being brought in contact with beer.[63]

Beer was undoubtedly a problem for the Church; but a far larger problem was that many of the villagers believed quite simply that poaching, at least for the pot, was not poaching, or theft, or covetousness at all: it was part of the Englishman's birthright, which had been unjustly taken away by the game laws. Moreover, although there was an inveterate tendency for men and women to show deference to their 'betters', deference had to be earned; and it only extended so far, when it came to game.

On Friday 3 March 1899 the *Sheffield Independent* reported the following sacrilegious event:

> At the Rotherham Borough Police Court yesterday, Isaac Bower of no fixed abode, was charged with breaking into and entering Thorpe Hesley church and schools on January 30th. The vicar (Rev. R. T. C. Slade) said that in consequence of an intimation he visited the church on the afternoon of January 30th, and found that a pane of glass in the vestry door had been broken. The door was unlocked, and a drawer of a table in the vestry was open. No damage had been done, and nothing was taken. He visited the schools prior to going to the church, and saw

---

63 *Manchester Courier and Lancashire General Advertiser*, Saturday 26 May 1888; *Sheffield Evening Telegraph* - Monday 1 October 1888; *Sheffield Independent*, Monday 01 October 1888.

that a window there had been broken. In reply to Mr. Hickmott solicitor, who defended, witness said there were no valuables in the church. Several witnesses were called, but there being no evidence to connect the prisoner with the offence, the case was dismissed.

LIBERALISM

In the General Election of 1880, the Liberal Party swept to power, after the turbulent 'Midlothian' campaign, in which Gladstone vigorously attacked the government of Benjamin Disraeli. One result of the victory was the Ground Game Act. Another was the Representation of the People Act of 1884 (also known as the Third Reform Act), which greatly extended the franchise. All men paying an annual rental of £10 and all those holding land valued at £10 now had the vote and the British electorate totalled over 5,500,000. At the same time, Rotherham became a parliamentary constituency, which the Liberals took and held until 1918.[64] A local branch of the Liberal party was established in Thorpe Hesley and Scholes by 1880:

> On Tuesday evening the annual business meeting of the Thorpe Hesley, Scholes, and Liberal Association, was held at the Red Lion Inn, Thorpe Hesley, near Rotherham. Mr. S. Jarvis presided, and there was good attendance. The chairman congratulated those present on the work which they had done during the past year. The meeting then proceeded to appoint officers for the next year. A general discussion on public matters afterwards took place, and the usual vote of thanks terminated the proceedings.[65]

TRADE UNIONS

As for the coalminers, there are reports of several mass meetings at the Old School Yard and elsewhere in Thorpe Hesley, notably in 1870, 1882 and 1885, which were held during strikes at local pits; but not everyone approved of trade

---

64 Gummer, 249.
65 *Barnsley Chronicle*, Saturday 4 September 1880.

unions. In particular, a Thorpe Hesley man wrote this letter to the Editor of the *Sheffield Independent* on Wednesday 25 October 1893.[66]

> There seem to be a number of jealous, carping spirits abroad at Thorpe Hesley, writing to yon under the nom de plumes of 'Crying Justice' and 'Justice'. 'Justice' asks if our local leaders are true to their cause? Let actions speak, for actions speak louder than words. What have these men done for the poor miners of this district during the present disastrous and prolonged struggle? Have they not promoted and provided free teas for hundreds of poor children? Have they not caused stones of flour innumerable to be distributed amongst the poorest households? Have they not given money in needy cases without publicly crying the good work they have done? Sir Walter Scott characterised calumny as the vile habit into which baser spirits sank of cutting honest throats by whispers. I would advise our leaders not to let these insinuations hinder them in the good work they are carrying on so nobly, but to press on with their labours—Yours truly A MINER BUT NOT A COMMITTEE MAN Thorpe Hesley, Oct. 23, 1893.

There were also certain outrages committed at Thorpe Hesley, in the name of trade unionism, which attracted the attentions of the national press. On Saturday 21 December 1861 two nailshops in Kirby Lane and Thorpe Street were blown up, by crude bombs made from tin cans and gunpowder. No-one was hurt, but there was considerable damage to property and John Hattersley and Charles Butcher were put out of business.

The background to this was that Hattersley was a foreman employed by a Mr Favell (or Flavell) of Westgate in Rotherham, who was in the horse-nail trade. Favell paid wages which were less than those recommended by the Nailmakers' Union, which had its headquarters in Belper but had a branch in Thorpe. The Union men had called a strike, which produced a hostile atmosphere in the

---

66 *Cork Examiner*, Tuesday 22 February 1870; *Sheffield Independent*, Thursday 13 April 1882; *Sheffield Daily Telegraph*, Tuesday 15 August 1882; *Sheffield Independent*, Saturday 10 October 1885.

The Jubilee Poacher

village. On 19 October 1861 Thomas Jenkinson had been asked by a Union man whether he intended to begin making nails for Favell. Jenkinson had confirmed that he did, once he had 'worked up his common iron'. Despite being told that he had 'better be on strike and have 8s from the box per week', Jenkinson had insisted that he intended to take the chance of work while he had it, to which the reply had been: 'If you do, it will be the worse for you'.

Men from Belper visited Thorpe on more than one occasion, to persuade the 'knobsticks' (blacklegs) to join the strike. As Butcher explained: 'the Union men wanted us to leave off work because we were working under them in prices'. The Unionists held meetings in local pubs, in particular on 28 October 1861, but the 'knobsticks' refused to attend. Men from Belper and Chesterfield who were present at this meeting were heard to vow that they would 'blow the b-----s up'. Later that night, someone placed a can of gunpowder in the chimney of Charles Butcher's workshop, so that it would explode next day when the fire was lit. On this occasion the 'infernal machine' was discovered in time and no damage was done. Hattersley and Butcher still refused to take industrial action; but, as we know, the bombers struck again on the Saturday before Christmas, this time successfully.

The jury was out for only forty minutes and returned to find all three prisoners guilty. The judge then sentenced each of them to the maximum penalty prescribed for the offence - fourteen years' penal servitude. The *Advertiser* reported that: 'The prisoners, who were confident of an acquittal, seemed to be completely overwhelmed by the result of the trial and sentence."[67] In view of the doubts surrounding the case, it is pleasing to report that the prisoners were released, and within months, as was reported, inter alia, in the *Norfolk News* on Saturday 24 May 1862.

> The three men sentenced to penal servitude for years at the last Yorkshire assizes for the trade outrage at Thorpe Hesley, near Sheffield, have been set at liberty. The evidence on the trial was very conflicting." That for the prosecution was apparently conclusive, but no fewer than seventeen

---

[67] This story was first published in *Aspects of Rotherham* ed Melvyn Jones (Wharncliffe Publishing Ltd, 1995): my article on *The Stirrings in Thorpe Hesley on Saturday Night*.

witnesses deposed to having seen one of the prisoners at Belper and another at Chesterfield, at the time when the outrage was perpetrated.

HOT WORK FOR THE POLICE

What sort of place was Thorpe Hesley? When I moved there from Chapeltown in 1979, I was warned by someone who lived in High Green that Thorpe itself was very nice but that the people were inclined to be 'cliquish' (which she pronounced 'clickish'). She meant, amongst other things, that they stuck together, and against the outside world; and there is some evidence that this was so in Ernest Dobson's day. The *Sheffield Daily Telegraph* for Tuesday 22 September 1857 reported the following incident under the heading 'Hot Work for the Police'.

> Rotherham Court House. Emma Parkin, Ellen Duke, and Ann Brook, all of Thorpe Hesley, were charged with assaulting and obstructing John Smalley and Christopher Stockdale, two police-officers, in the execution of their duty. Mr. Clark Branson, of Sheffield, defended Mrs. Parkin. On Tuesday last Smalley went to the house of Caroline Bamforth, at Thorpe Hesley, to execute a warrant of ejectment. He first went at half-past eleven, and then allowed her until half past one o'clock to get her effects ready for removal. At that time he again found there were no preparations for removal, and another half-hour was then allowed; but still no signs of commencement.
>
> The three defendants were then in the house, and when the officer began to remove the furniture himself, obstructed him, and ultimately a regular row took place, and Stockdale was called in to assist. During the scuffle Smalley, by some mischance, got his fingers entangled in Mrs. Parkin's teeth, the effects of which constituted the principal ingredient in the assault. He likewise lost some of his hair. As the disturbance increased, different people were asked to come in and assist the officers, but instead of doing this they impeded them all they could.
>
> A dispute had lately arisen about the property, and Jenkinson said it had been left to him the lately deceased owner, who was a relative. The will, he said, he had destroyed; but the Parkins, who considered they

The Jubilee Poacher

had equal claim to it, did not believe this, and were now taking steps to investigate the matter in a higher court. Mrs. Bamforth used to live in a house of her own, but she left it in April last, and about that time came live with Mrs. Parkin, in consequence of Mr. Parkin and her having had a difference and separated. Since then they had, however, become reconciled, and Mrs. Bamforth had gone to live with Jenkinson, and so she was living when the warrant of ejectment was taken out in her name. She never had been the tenant, and a gross and wicked attempt had been made upon the bench in getting them to issue the warrant.

A report in the *Sheffield Daily Telegraph* a week later provided further details:

The town had been in commotion all the preceding evening in consequence of the ejectment process, and the defendants were endeavouring to keep up the excitement. The two officers (Stockdale and Smalley) endeavoured to persuade them to go home, but they refused, and commenced throwing stones and otherwise assaulted the officers... Benjamin Copley was distinctly seen to throw a stone at P.C. Stockdale, and when the latter attempted to take him into custody the crowd prevented him.

In the 1890s, it was recorded in *White's Directory* that Thorpe Hesley was 'mostly in Wentworth polling district of the Hallamshire division of Yorkshire, but partly in the Rotherham division'. It was also stated that the village was divided between different authorities and jurisdiction for ecclesiastical purposes; and one cannot help wondering whether these divisions did not encourage the feeling that inhabitants of the village lived 'on the edge' of society, where some must have felt like outsiders.

IMPROVEMENTS

There was a feeling in the late 19th century – as there was for some in 1997 - that 'things could only get better.' The economy had grown enormously since the 'hungry forties' and the poacher James Harker was well aware of the reason:

Some men are now blaming machinery for their troubles [but] you cannot place any Restriction on the ingenuity of man. If you Do, and try to Prevent these developments, what a mistake we should make. The benefits through Machinery are Greater than the injuries. Suppose I Cary you Back to the old Coaching Days - which I well Remember and often whish I could Forget. It took four Days to Travel from London to Liverpool. Now they Do it in a few hours. I Have seen Coaches snowed up for Days. What sort of a should we be in to Day if we Had no Steam or Machinery?

Thorpe Hesley was more prosperous in the 1890s than it had been in the 1840s. Whereas it had been the home of 'nailers and agriculturists', it was now the home of farm labourers and coalminers, but there were many other trades. *White's Directory* for 1891 mentioned 3 pits, 9 pubs and beerhouses, 18 shopkeepers, (including a draper, a pork butcher and boot and shoe maker, a clog maker, and Ezra Smith who was a grocer and wine and spirit merchant, with branches in Wentworth and Harley), 14 farmers (including two women, Mrs Sarah Burgin and Mrs H. Earnshaw), and still two nail manufacturers, one of whom had diversified into the manufacture of bolts, screws and marine engineering. There were also tradesmen, including at least one builder, joiner and carpenter (Frank Jenkinson), blacksmith,. The total population was stated to be 2,178 in 1881.

Change came in many forms, and communications was one. By 1891 there were three railway stations within two miles of the village – those at Chapeltown, Ecclesfield and Grange Lane, while Thorpe Hesley itself had a Post and Money Order Office, run by the grocer Henry Butcher, with a 'wall letter box' on the corner of Barnsley lane, which was cleared by 6.10 p.m. daily, except on Sundays, and there were Telegraph Offices in Chapeltown and Kimberworth.

It had come to be recognised that workers of all kinds needed time off for holidays and leisure. Public parks and private clubs were set up, for example cycling clubs, which are mentioned with such enthusiasm in Joseph Harker's 'A Victorian Poacher.' The first cycling club in Rotherham formed in 1879.[68] We can see evidence of progress in this area in the illustrations which I have included

---

68 Gummer, 129.

in this book. In compiling them, I was struck how, in the decades considered, the drawing becomes accompanied by the photograph, and we start to see pictures of people enjoying themselves, at the local equivalent of the sea-side, or on an outing by bus [see illustrations 7 & 12]. At the same time, for obvious reasons, I never came across a photograph of the poacher at work,

An example of the improvements in living conditions which occurred at this time featured in the *Sheffield Daily Telegraph* on Thursday 14 July 1904.

DUKE OF NORFOLK AND THORPE HESLEY GIFT OF A PUBLIC RECREATION GROUND

On Tuesday evening a well-attended public meeting was held at the Ball Inn, Thorpe Hesley Bar.[69] Mr. Ernest Walker, Thorncliffe Collieries, presided. Mr. Ben Chapman read a letter from Mr. Coverdale agent to the Duke of Norfolk, stating that his Grace had been pleased to set apart about three acres land at Hesley Bar for a public recreation ground for the use and benefit of the inhabitants of that district.

Many other examples could be cited: among them, Boston Castle and Clifton House, both of which now belong to Rotherham Council. The first was leased from the Earl of Effingham in 1876, the second was purchased in 1891; but perhaps the best example of the phenomenon is Elsecar Park, now part of Barnsley. In 1910, a local amateur photographer, Herbert Parkin, took some photographs of the reservoir there and sent them to the *Sheffield Star* under the caption 'Elsecar-by-the-Sea' – though it is around 100 miles from the sea (about as far as one can get in Britain). However, despite the geography, the name caught on, and a thriving tourism business was established. The Hoyland council decided to create the public park to take advantage of the influx; and the name is still used, 'jokingly', to this day. [see again illustration 7].

---

69 So called because this was where users of the turnpike paid a toll. In 1825 receipts at the local toll gates had been: Grange Lane Bar £15/17/2d; Masborough Bar, £214/3/9d; Hesley Bar, £154/2/5d; High Green Bar, £109/7/5d. See illustration 13.

Three

The Law

The Background

The game laws had a long history in England. The Normans introduced new forest laws after 1066, whose savage nature is well known. These had long fallen into disuse by the close of the Middle Ages. During the Civil War and Commonwealth, what remained of the royal forests was taken over by the Long Parliament, which repealed many forest laws, and park walls were often thrown down, allowing 'poaching' to proceed largely unchecked. After 1660 the game laws came back with the Cavaliers; and a gentleman's 'game privilege', based on a high land qualification, was introduced. Shooting game was confined to the large landowners, esquires, knights, and their gamekeepers.[70] The gamekeepers were given powers of law enforcement.

In 1723 the notorious 'Black Act' criminalized trespassers who disguised themselves with blackened faces, especially those engaged in poaching on Waltham Chase. It provided capital punishment for over two hundred new offences; and it was regularly renewed, eventually becoming permanent in 1758. In 1770 the Night Poaching Act, 'laid on the lash' In William Cobbett's phrase), by criminalizing poaching, armed or unarmed, between an hour after

---

70 The *Leeds Intelligencer*, 23 and 30 October 1820, contains warnings posted by Gascoigne, in relation to his estates near Leeds.

sunset and an hour before sunrise. It provided for summary trial before a single magistrate, not less than three months' imprisonment for a first offence, and public whipping and not less than six months' imprisonment for the second. An Act of 1800 provided that 'persons at large at night', armed with nets or 'other offensive weapon' (for example a bludgeon) with 'intent to kill game' should be classified as 'rogues and vagabonds', and as such be whipped, imprisoned for two years or impressed into the army or navy. Gamekeepers and manorial servants were empowered to seize nets and equipment without warrant.

The French Revolution led to new legal measures, even harsher than the Black Act, as the landowners in Parliament, by far the most important interest represented there, battened down the hatches, for fear that Jacobin principles might produce revolution in England. Poachers came to be regarded as politically dangerous, as well as a social menace. Lord Ellenborough's Act of 1803 created ten new capital felonies, for example resisting lawful arrest. The Night Poaching Act of 1816 mandated 7 years' transportation for any person caught at night in any forest, chase, park, wood, plantation, close, or other open or enclosed ground, having in his possession 'any net, gun, bludgeon or offensive weapon'. Sir Samuel Romilly claimed that, if this measure had been fully enforced, it would have enabled the courts to transport half the rural population to Australia.[71]

These new laws had teeth, despite the absence of a police force. Landowners were allowed to set mantraps and spring-guns to deter and punish the poacher; but sadly these infernal machines sometimes caught innocent trespassers and uninvited guests, as well as culprits, and as a result became unpopular. For example, on Thursday 31 May 1821, the *Public Ledger and Daily Advertiser* reported as follows:

> On Friday last, as a young woman of the name of Kay, living at the house of Mr. Brown, of Ganstead, Yorkshire, was going in the morning about eight o'clock to gather eggs, as usual, her gown caught hold of a mantrap; and in rushing forward to escape the trap, she came in contact with

---

71 Hopkins, 78-80.

the wire of a spring-gun, which went off, and lodged the contents in her thigh, upwards of 40 shot corns. Medical assistance was sent for, and about 13 of the shots extracted. She is in a fair way of recovery.

In the early 19th century many landowners joined voluntary associations for the purpose of sharing the burden and expense of detecting and prosecuting crime. A prominent example was the Wentworth Association for the Prosecution of Felons, of which the Earl Fitzwilliam was a prominent member.[72] These associations were concerned with all types of crime; but poaching was certainly prominent. It was only in the 1850s that they became redundant, when country police forces and prosecutors were formed and appointed. Local landowners continued to maintain keepers of various kinds.

With the return of peace after 1815 there was some degree of liberalisation. The Black Act was repealed in 1823, and in the following years capital punishment for felonies against property was replaced, first with transportation and then (from the 1860s) with penal servitude. Most importantly perhaps, an Act of 1827 prohibited the use by the landowner of mantraps and spring-guns.

We can see that the liberalisation was relative, if we consult the first edition of Archbold's *Pleading and Evidence in Criminal Cases*, 1822 (the modern prisoner's Bible). After explaining that, at common law, it was not possible to prosecute someone for larceny of 'animals in which there is no property, as of beasts that are *ferae naturae*,[73] and unreclaimed, such as deer, hare and conies', the author went on to explain that there were many kinds of statutory offences which the prosecutor could use when framing an indictment, for example, when the poacher went after ground game, deer, pheasants, and fish; and he even made specific reference to suitable charges which could be used in the case of swans, hawks, and oysters.

Not everyone was in favour of change. There were even those who opposed the Act which prohibited the use of spring-guns and mantraps as 'an attack on gentlemen who wished to preserve their plantations and woods'; and as contrary to the principle that it was better to prevent a crime than to punish it. One

---

72 Still in existence, though its functions are now purely social.
73 *Of a wild nature.*

speaker asserted that 'the bloody battles between poachers and preservers of game scarcely ever took place where guns and traps were set.'

In the general election of 1831, the Whigs were returned with a majority of 131 and Earl Grey formed a government. This enacted a number of progressive measures apart from the well known Great Reform Act of 1832. Among them was the Game Act of 1831, which abolished the 'qualifications' established in 1671. It is interesting to note that Lord Wharncliffe (the owner of a large estate in South Yorkshire) spoke in Parliament in favour of abolition.[74]

According to the poacher James Harker, the 'Hungry Forties' were aptly named:

> The mid-1840s were wretched times. Sheep Stealing, Highway Robbery and Burglary were common. It was not Safe to go out after Dark. If a Man stole a Sheep he Had 14 years Transportation. If hunger made a man go into the woods to get a pheasant, he too would get fourteen years. Two men in Oadby Had 14 years - Jack Baurn, Bill Devonport - for attempting to take Pheasants in Tugley Wood in 1847, so this is No Dream.

In the general election of 1859 the Conservatives were returned with a majority of 59 and the Earl of Derby formed a government. In 1862 the Poaching Prevention Act 1862 allowed police officers to stop and search anyone on the road for evidence of poaching, and confiscate nets, snares and guns.[75] Some MPs wanted to repeal the new Act, others went further and wanted to repeal all the statutes which made poaching illegal.[76] One such gave three reasons. The first was that poaching was driven by a natural instinct, which was the love of sport. This reflected a common feeling, expressed even by the Rev Gilbert White in his *Natural History of Selborne* (1802): 'the temptation [to poach] is irresistible, for most men are sportsmen by nature'.[77] The second reason was that men would inevitably be tempted to poach, because of "the hope of gain, strengthened by the

---

74 Hansard, HL Deb 06 April 1827 vol 17 cc 268-70.
75 Chenevix Trench, 181-2.
76 *HC Deb 17 March 1863 vol 169 cc1554-731554*
77 Quoted by E.P.Thompson, in *Whigs & Hunters*, p 162.

greater facilities which now existed for getting game to market." The third reason was that game was at present being 'over-preserved', in places bordering upon densely-populated districts. In addition, it was good for the animal kingdom that it should be properly culled from time to time, and game was so abundant now that the gamekeepers were not capable of doing the job by themselves!

Conservatives opposed repeal because 'the important principle at stake was not the preservation of game, but the preservation of life, public morality and the rights of property'. Several MPs thought that the Act was very necessary, citing the opinion of chief constables in the midlands and northern districts, that the crime of poaching had assumed a new shape. Poaching was now 'the work of organized bands, who went out at night, and after sweeping the preserves, returned home with their spoil along the highway and despatched it from the next railway station; openly defying the constables who thus saw them go to the covers and saw them return with the result of their nocturnal depredations'.

THE GROUND GAME ACT OF 1880

During his barnstorming Midlothian campaign of 1880, Gladstone complained that (with a few exceptions) the aristocracy and landowners had failed the nation. He and his Liberal Party won a stunning victory in the General Election that year and secured a majority of 51 in the House of Commons. A Liberal Government was formed, and a Ground Game Bill was proposed in the Queen's Speech, which would confer on farmers, at long last, the 'unalienable, concurrent right' to shoot hares and rabbits on their land.[78]

Hopkins, the author of *The Long Affray*, was concerned to portray the history of poaching in the 19th century as part of the class struggle; but he damned the Ground Game Act of 1880 with faint praise. In his view, it was a limited measure, since it simply meant that the tenant farmer shared the right to take the ground game with the landowner: it did nothing to legalise poaching by the landless farm labourer, miner or industrial worker. In any event, as the *Daily Telegraph* pointed out, it did nothing to alter the law with regard to pheasants and partridges, which were what 'the Big Shots' were chiefly interested in. Moreover, the penalties for poaching remained disproportionate.

---

78 Hopkins, 268.

However, the Act of 1880 did make a difference so far as Ernest Dobson was concerned. Prior to the change in the law, he was always charged with trespassing on land belonging to one of the local landowners – Earl Fitzwilliam, the Duke of Norfolk or the Earl of Wharncliffe. But afterwards, he was sometimes charged with trespassing on land in the occupation of one of the local farmers – Joseph Pilley, William Senior, Joseph Cooper, or George Merryman - or on land occupied by Newton Chambers & Co., in connection with their enterprises or on land belonging to the industrialist E.L.W.Bellhouse at Grenoside. This meant that, when he went after ground game, the 'victims' (and the private prosecutors) came from a wider range of society. So far as pheasants were concerned, Dobson was charged on one occasion as having poached on land over which Michael Ellison had the shooting rights, rather than an interest in the land; but whether Dobson even knew this, is open to question.

GUN CONTROL

In contrast to the United States, we have had strict legislation controlling guns for a very long time; but it was not always so. The classic statement of the position in English common law is contained in Blackstone's *Commentaries on the Laws of England*, in particular Volume One *On the Rights of Persons*, published in 1765. There Blackstone states that the subject has three principal and absolute rights – to enjoyment of life and limb, health and reputation; liberty; and property – and five auxiliary or subordinate rights. These are (1) the powers and privileges of Parliament; (2) the limitation of the King's prerogative; (3) the right to apply to the courts for redress of injuries; (4) the right to petition the King, or either House of Parliament, for the redress of grievances; and last but by no means least (5) that of having arms for their defence, suitable to their condition or degree, and such as are allowed by law.

However, by the time Blackstone wrote his *Commentaries*, the right provided for in the Bill of Rights had already been modified by the Disarming Acts of 1716 and 1725 and by the Act of Proscription of 1746, which served to suppress the Jacobite Rebellions and demilitarise the Highlands and Islands of Scotland. In the early 19th century, when it was widely feared that a 'crime wave' was sweeping across the country, fuelled by soldiers and sailors returning from the Napoleonic

Wars, Parliament enacted the Vagrancy Act of 1824, the Night Poaching Acts of 1828 and 1844 and various Game Acts, starting in 1831. These all had the effect of controlling the possession of firearms, at least by the 'lower orders'. However, Ernest Dobson was never prosecuted for having a gun without a licence.

The Machinery of Justice

In the 19th century minor offences were dealt with in the Magistrates Courts, or 'Petty Sessions', popularly known as the 'Police Courts', or 'Petty Sessions', while more serious offences were heard by the magistrates at the Quarter Sessions or else at the Assizes. There, the evidence was considered twice, first by a Grand Jury of between 14 and 23 and then by a Petty Jury of 12 'good men and true'.

The main changes in sentencing in the decades prior to 1877 were that an Act of 1853 had replaced transportation with penal servitude. This involved hard labour, for six or more hours a day, on the treadmill, shot drill or the crank machine. The treadmill speaks for itself: prisoners were treated like pet hamsters are today. Shot drill involved moving cannonballs from one pile to another. The crank was a device which forced four large cups or ladles through sand inside a drum. Male prisoners sometimes had to turn the handle around 14,000 times a day; and the warder could make the task harder by tightening and adjusting the screw, which gave rise to the use of the term as slang for a prison officer.

Wakefield Prison

When Ernest Dobson was sentenced to imprisonment, or had to go to prison because he had failed to pay a fine, he served the time in Wakefield Prison, once known as Wakefield House of Correction. In the 18th century, the place had an evil reputation. The great reformer, John Howard, visited it in 1774 and wrote:

WEST RIDING, WAKEFIELD.

This prison is unfortunately built upon low ground; so it is damp and exposed to floods. Four of the wards are spacious, but all the wards are made vary offensive by sewers. Prison and Court are out of sight from the keeper's house, though adjoining; and some prisoners have escaped.

> They are now let out to the Court only half an hour in the day. The wards are dirty. A prison on ground so low as this requires the utmost attention to cleanliness. Allowance: two-pence a day; little or no employment

Things had improved a great deal by 1850 and, during the second half of the nineteenth century Wakefield Prison became known as a pioneer establishment. There can be little doubt that it was the most efficiently administered of the County Gaols at the time of its handing over to the Prison Commissioners in 1877. The outstanding feature of a further change was the introduction of industrial employment for prisoners on a large scale, in place of the monotonous and unproductive drudgery of the crank and the treadmill. The West Riding Justices became profoundly sceptical of the value of penal labour and in Mr. Edward Shepherd and Captain Godfrey Armitage they were served by enlightened and progressive men. Their views on the employment of prisoners gradually gained general acceptance.

There are records showing Ernest Dobson arriving at the prison on around twelve occasions, and each time a clerk recorded particulars of the court which had committed him, the offence for which he had been committed and the sentence, the kind of education he had received, his age, height and the colour of his hair, his trade or occupation and any distinguishing marks or characteristics, his religion and place of birth, and the number of previous convictions. This they seem to have done meticulously, though not always consistently, and when he came to be released, a clerk also recorded the date. Thus although the record is almost certainly incomplete, and the details for the years 1878-81 are impossible to decipher, we can tell that he spent at least four months in the jail in 1879; 12 months in 1882; three months in 1883; 28 days in 1890; 1 day, a further 5 days and then a further month in 1891; one month in 1892; 28 days in 1896; one month in 1899; one month in 1895; and (perhaps) 2 months in 1906 (the record here once again being very obscure). This makes a total of almost two and a half years, spent in jail overall.[79] This is not perhaps a great deal of time, compared to a lifetime; but it is long enough when we consider how trivial the vast majority of those offences appeared to be, in Dobson's own mind.

---

79 The shortness of some of these periods is accounted for by the fact that Dobson, or someone else, sometimes paid off his fines.

Four

Attitudes

The Rotherham Case, 1865

There is a kind of counter-culture attached to poaching. Some Englishmen have long argued that they have a fundamental right to take game, whatever laws may prohibit this; and, there was an affray in the Rotherham area in 1865 which perfectly illustrates this. The leader of the poachers here was a puddler,[80] while two were colliers, two were labourers, and one was a 'navvy'. There was a battle between gamekeepers and poachers; and a gamekeeper was killed; but there was a question as to who had attacked first, and (at least in some minds) whether this involved murder or 'merely' manslaughter. The *Daily Telegraph*, and the *Glasgow Herald* for Wednesday 27 December 1865 each carried the story.

TRIAL OF POACHERS FOR MURDER.

The trial of David Booth, William Sykes, Aaron Savage, John Teale, John Bentcliffe and Henry Bone, on the charge of murdering William Lilly, gamekeeper on the Silverwood estate at Ravenfield, was commenced on Thursday, at the Leeds Assizes, before Mr. Justice Shee, and did not close till Saturday.

---

80 A person who puddles clay or, in this case (probably) iron.

The Jubilee Poacher

> The alleged murder occurred in this way. The deceased and three other watchers went out to protect game in Silverwood, and about ten o'clock at night seven men were seen in the wood setting snares. The watchers rushed upon them, and Lilley, who was foremost, was struck down by a blow from a stick, and then belaboured on the head and body. He was fearfully injured, and died the day following. Sykes, Teale, and Bone were identified by the watchers, but the chief evidence against them was that of Robert Woodhouse, an approver.[81]

The Coroner said

> Certainly, this was an enormous crime, a very sad and melancholy case, one which I fear will be repeated month after month as long as there are game laws in existence. I think it a pity that any man should lose his life for the sake of game. Nevertheless the game law is the law of the land. The sooner we can get rid of all laws that lead to these quarrels, the better it will be.

The lawyer appearing for the murdered man's relatives did not agree. He protested: 'That is a matter for the legislature;' but the coroner replied

> No doubt it is, but I still think we are justified in expressing our opinion that laws which cannot be maintained in their integrity, nor cannot be carried out except at the risk of killing either poachers or gamekeepers, cannot be very good laws.'[82]

During the course of the trial at Leeds Assizes, the Q.C. for the prosecution told the jury:

---

81 A person who confesses to committing a crime and gives evidence against his or her accomplices.
82 *London Evening Standard*, Saturday 14 October 1865.

The case itself arose out one of those unfortunate night affrays which take place in this and other parts of the country between those who are the appointed and lawful guardians and protectors and watchers of game, and persons who think it proper to give their time and employ themselves in the habitual practice of night poaching. Whatever may be said in reference to the policy of the laws which protect game, I would ask you to be guided and guarded by those higher considerations which seek for security of the subject, and according to which life, if that has been taken, cannot and shall not be sacrificed.

In his summing-up the judge told the jury that there was no element in the case which' could possibly reduce the charge from murder to manslaughter (and thereby avoid the death penalty); but this was precisely what they did with four of the poachers; and they also recommended one found guilty of murder to mercy, and acquitted the other two.[83]

The Judge disapproved, and said so; but the *Sheffield and Rotherham Independent* commended the jury: 'The law was the judge's. Common sense was the jury's.' The paper conceded that night poaching was 'very wrong'; but,

When it comes to a question of losing a few partridges and hares, or risking human life, men cannot consent to weigh one against the other... A man doesn't commonly resist to death to save his house being robbed... Yet the armament of the keepers proves that they went about the preservation of game in a way quite different to that used by watchers of other property. Are we come to that state of savagery that men in lawful employment are allowed to use the brutal and lawless weapons of the most dangerous felons?

The Sheffield *Daily Telegraph* condemned all those concerned:

The behaviour has been unEnglish on all sides - the poachers acting like savages, the keepers like hares, and the employer like a snob.

---

83 Hopkins, 240-2.

THE COUNTER CULTURE

As we have noted, William the Conqueror created new royal forests, and invented a new system of forest law which protected game from the attentions of the common people and reserved hunting rights for his new French-speaking aristocracy. During the late Middle Ages, poaching became romanticised in English literature, in the stories and ballads of Robin Hood. During the English Civil Wars of 1642-49 and under the English Republic of 1649-60 the Levellers and Diggers produced pamphlets arguing that the Englishman was entitled to rid himself of 'the Norman Yoke'.[84] The old game laws were swept away, and many park walls were thrown down.

As we have also seen, there was a reaction after 1660, which saw the introduction of the gentleman's 'game privilege'. This excluded not only landless peasants but tenant farmers and the majority of yeomen farmers too; and only a very small group of people were now allowed to shoot game legally. This created the potential for a class war, especially since it also allowed the upper classes to appoint gamekeepers.[85]

Not everyone was in agreement with the new game laws, introduced by the Cavalier Parliament, and massively reinforced from the 1720s by a series of 'Black Acts.' A letter written to *The Gentleman's Magazine* in 1753 argued that 'Game Laws are contrary to the liberties of mankind. God himself, the Creator of all things, gave man a right to kill and eat the birds of the air, the beasts of the field etc'.[86] This view was echoed in a popular ballad which criticised those who enclosed the commons, and re-modelled villages in order to improve the view.

> The law locks up the hapless felon
> who steals the goose from off the common,
> but lets the greater felon loose
> who steals the common from the goose.

---

84 E.g. Christopher Hill on the Norman Yoke in *Puritanism and Revolution*, 1958.
85 Hopkins, 63.
86 Chenevix Trench, 125.

The criticism of 18th century landlords was also summarised in Goldsmith's famous poem *The Deserted Village*

> His seat, where solitary sports are seen
> Indignant, spurns the cottage from the green…
> Where then, ah where! shall poverty reside
> To 'scape the pressure of contiguous pride?

Goldsmith also asked 'What can be more arbitrary than to talk of preserving game which, when defined, means nothing more than that the poor shall abstain from what the rich have taken a fancy to for themselves?'

A favourable impression of the common poacher was conveyed to a popular audience by *The Lincolnshire Poacher*, a folk song first printed in York in 1776, the year of the Declaration of Independence in America.

> When I was bound apprentice in famous Lincolnshire,
> Full well I serv'd my master, for more than seven year,
> Till I took up to poaching, as you shall quickly hear.
> Oh, 'tis my delight on a shining night, in the season of the year.
>
> As me and my companions was setting off a snare,
> 'Twas then we spied the gamekeeper – for him we did not care,
> For we can wrestle and fight, my boys, and jump o'er anywhere.
> Oh, 'tis my delight on a shining night, in the season of the year.

During the course of the 19th century the game laws were attacked by the pamphleteer William Cobbett, the Radical and free trader John Bright, the Liberal Unionist Joseph Chamberlain, the Liberal Lloyd George [see illustration 20], and the Socialist William Morris; but perhaps the most startling judgment was given by the 19th century archivist and historian, Sir Francis Palgrave, K.H., F.R.S., (1788 – 1861). He traced their origin to the Vikings:

> The conquerors gave the widest constitution to the law of property: air, water and earth, all were to be theirs, fowl, fish and beast of chase, where the arrow could fly the dog could draw, or the net could fall – sportsmen, huntsmen, the Danish lords appropriated to themselves all woodland and water, copse and grove, river, marsh and mere.[87]

UPPER CLASS ATTITUDES

Not everyone agreed. In particular, the landowners violently disagreed with idea of law reform in a liberal direction. For Cobbett's opponents, trespassing in pursuit of game was a crime, and violence, let alone murder or attempted murder, must attract the full rigours of the law. Thus the *Quarterly Review* in 1820, was highly critical of the proposal to repeal the Black Act 'we should never consent to disarm justice of any of the terrors which properly belong to it'.

Harry Hopkins gives an extraordinary example of the conflict between the reformist and the conservative view, by pointing to two gravestones erected in memory of the same person. This was a poacher named Charles Smith, who was executed in 1822 for attempting to murder a gamekeeper. One gravestone remembers him as a martyr, citing the fact that he 'suffered at Winchester for resisting by firearms his apprehension by the gamekeeper of Lord Palmerston, looking after what is called Game. The other stone tells us that Smith 'fired at close range the whole contents of his gun into [the gamekeeper's] body.'[88]

In the high Victorian period, the upper classes tended to think that the lower orders were tainted with original sin and too often succumbed to the 'insidious perils' of the 'beerhouse'. Later in the century, in Galsworthy's *The Country House* Lady Malden remarks 'I've no sympathy with poachers. So many of them do it just for the love of the sport.'[89] The following article appeared in *The Globe* for Saturday 20 February 1897.

---

87 *The History of Normandy and of England*, volume 1, Francis Palgrave, (1851, Pyrrhus Press, 2014)
88 Hopkins, 2-3.
89 Hopkins, 296-300.

Stephen Cooper

THE POACHER'S WIFE.

It is a curious fact that the British poacher almost invariably has a sick wife and an extensive progeny on the very verge of starvation. These poor creatures, it is true, usually present, as he does himself, every appearance of robust health, nor are they unknown visitors to the public-house. But should the bread-winner be caught in the act of appropriating property, whether furred or feathered, to which he has no legal right, his household instantly falls into a most distressful condition. At Barnsley the other day, one of these self-sacrificing men pathetically pleaded that he was wholly influenced by consideration for his poor wife. Being out of work, he could not provide her with food, and he therefore set forth to obtain just one rabbit, to save her from starvation… In most of these cases, the "clemming" wife is purely mythical; if she really existed, the readiest means of keeping her from starving would be to annex provisions at shops. Of course, that would be equally dishonest, but it would have the merit, at all events, of affording quicker relief to the hungry wife. On the whole, the magistrates appear to gauge the situation correctly by rarely giving heed to her pitiable condition.

THE POACHER

We are fortunate in having the views of a poacher, albeit not a Yorkshireman. Although he was not a learned man, and spent his whole adult life in the pursuit of game in the Midlands, rather than in the groves of Academe, James Hawker (1836–1921) wrote a journal in 1904. Harker tells us that as a young man, he had a regular income from soldiering – that was how acquired his first gun – while in later life he worked as a cobbler, in a hosiery factory, at a leather works, as a groom and as a farmworker; but, more importantly, he tells us about his career in poaching.

Harker explains that he first became a poacher because he and his family lived in poverty, but stayed a poacher largely for the sport, and because he could make extra money that way. He often hunted alone or in a pair, but his description of catching rabbits with a long net tells us that he sometimes went out with a gang, and in the nature of it, this would have been an armed gang. On the other hand, his advice was always to avoid confrontations with gamekeepers if one could, for example by watching for crows or blackbirds when in a spinney – 'if they fly over, you will soon know if any [keeper] is in it.' He also remarked 'I shan't say Don't Poach, but do be careful.' Another piece of advice was to sit still.

Harker was a man of the Left. Though it was many years before he gained the vote, he was eventually elected to the school-board in Oadby, Leicestershire, and in 1894 he was elected to the parish council. He kept photographs of Gladstone and Bradlaugh in his diary, and ultimately joined both a trade union and the Labour Party. He wrote this about the Tories:

There's too much of Follow My Leader about the Tory Party. When will the Working Men Send their Own Class to Rule? The Tories are only doing what we Refuse to Do which is Watch Our Own Interests.

Harker's view of the game laws was that they were a means whereby 'the Class' (that is to say the Landowners and Squires) oppressed the Poor. He also though they were hypocritical, because in practice everybody poached – including people who were not poor, other landowners, and even policemen and gamekeepers – but it was only the poor and downtrodden who were prosecuted and punished. At the same time, Harker did not hate the Tories personally. He sat with them on the school-board, and even made friends with some of them.

By and large, Harker seems to have 'got away' with it, in the sense that he was seldom apprehended and sometimes escaped from custody (being a fit man and a good runner, as well as a regular cyclist). When he was brought before the court, he was sometimes acquitted and seldom punished heavily, the punishment usually being a fine, which he neglected to pay. He was only sent to prison once ('for getting a poor old widow woman some sticks, as she had no coal' – or so he claimed).

One might almost say that, from Harker's point of view, crime did pay, since it is clear that he could make a profit, especially from catching hares; but his main motivation seems to have been sheer enjoyment of the chase, which was not spoilt by any feeling of guilt, because he did not think that what he was doing was wrong, or ought to be unlawful, let alone criminal. For the same reasons he did not think much of his opponents, be they gamekeepers or policemen:

> My biggest Enemies - Keepers and Police - don't really worry a poacher so much as Courting Couples. They generally get into a nice corner or nook where they think they are out of all Danger of being Heard. But they forget that a Poacher may be near. If you only knew what I have Heard in the Lanes, you would laugh. I have heard Promises made, but not kept...

Modern Views

In the 20th century the historian G.M. Trevelyan and the popular writer Harry Hopkins agreed with Harker: the battle between poachers and gamekeepers was essentially a class war. This view is also apparent in D.H. Lawrence's *Lady Chatterley's Lover*, first published privately in 1928. The novel was about many things (including sex); but it was also about class. So, the gamekeeper Mellors says at one point that he hates 'the impudence of class', whilst the baronet Sir Clifford Chatterley is finally so shocked and disgusted by his wife's affair with Mellors that he tells her 'My God, you ought to be wiped from the face of the earth'; but Sir Clifford is portrayed as an impotent member of a dying breed, whose place is usurped by Mellor, the gamekeeper - a new and virile member of the working class.

In 1956-7 there was a BBC television series about a country bumpkin called *Nathaniel Titlark*. Titlark, played by Bernard Miles, was also a poacher and therefore a lawbreaker. Now, in those days, all Westerns, most dramas, and certainly all children's programmes portrayed the world in black and white terms. There were cowboys and Red Indians, cops and robbers, heroes and villains, and you were not expected to sympathise with the second category. It was a novel experience to do so, and to be encouraged to do so – because Titlark was a loveable rogue.

In *Whigs and Hunters* (1975), E.P. Thompson mounted a sustained attack on Sir Robert Walpole and the Whigs. A great advocate of the 'moral economy',

The Jubilee Poacher

Thompson attempted to show that Walpole's period as Prime Minister (1721-42) was an age of oppression and corruption, rather than one of political stability, as J.H.Plumb had argued.[90] For Thompson the 18th century game laws were used to legitimise the property rights of the landowner, at the expense of the landless peasant.

Barry Hines's novel *The Gamekeeper* was first published in 1975 and was set (more or less) in that time. The gamekeeper George Purse lives and works on an anonymous 'north country ducal estate' but Hines came from Hoyland Common, Barnsley, which adjoins Wentworth, and the descriptions in the novel, of 'the Big House', the estate village, the surrounding countryside, the park with lakes and gardens and above all the folly known as the Needle's Eye, all make it clear that the scene of the action must be Earl Fitzwilliam's Wentworth Woodhouse estate, in all but name. (Hines had set his *Kestrel for a Knave* (1968) in Barnsley).

George Purse is working-class, having previously worked as a steelworker, and he considers himself lucky to have obtained a post as one of the gamekeepers on the estate. He enjoys the outdoor life, but his position means that he has to keep himself to himself, and his two young sons are given the cold shoulder at school, because of their Dad's occupation. By acting as a gamekeeper, George is seen to be siding with the landowners and against the workers (who, if they participate in a shoot, do so as beaters). George is loyal to his master and does not approve of poachers. He thinks they deserve the sentences which are handed down by the courts; but the other point of view is given space. A friend asks: "Trespassing? And where did they get their land in the first place, any road? They just grabbed it, didn't they? Or the King dished it out to courtiers and pimps and royal bastards born on the wrong side of the blanket." Barry Hines portrays George Purse as a man who is not wholly at ease with himself.

Finally, in her novel *The Shooting Party* (written in 1980 but set in 1913) Isabel Colegate included a character called Tom Harker – and it is surely no coincidence that the surname was the same as that of the real poacher James Harker (see above). Tom Harker is employed on or near a large estate; but, unlike Barry

---

90   *Whigs & Hunters*, (Penguin, 1990, originally published 1975).

Hines's hero, he is also a poacher. In one scene, he catches a rabbit for his pot and we are also told how he catches it, kills it and cooks it, under the noses of his employers. Like James Harker, Tom is not a drinker, because he 'has seen too much what it can do to a man'; and, like James, he has radical views. We are told that he is both an admirer of Lloyd George and very critical of the game laws. Yet Tom is also loyal to his master, an admirer of the sporting prowess of his 'betters', and patriotic. When he is accidentally shot at the end of the novel, he and his master recite the Lord's Prayer together. On his death bed, his last words are 'God Save the British Empire!'

FEMALE POACHERS

There were very few prosecutions involving female poachers; but there were some. The *Sheffield Daily Telegraph* for Wednesday 30 September 1857 carried the following story concerning an event which had occurred not far from Thorpe Hesley, and in one of the places where Ernest Dobson habitually poached.[91]

> "Not take a rabbit doing damage in my own garden!"
>
> So gasped out the female poacher at Sheffield.
>
> 'No', says the Yorkshire magistrate.
>
> "What, not if they enter my husband's garden and destroy his vegetables!"
>
> Rabbits have a funny way of nibbling all the green produce within reach of their greedy mouths. It would seem that the Yorkshire justice thought it a hard case, and he let off the woman upon the payment of 10s. 6d. for costs. This misguided woman had ventured beyond her garden, and had placed a trap in an adjacent fence. No doubt she was off her property and

---

[91] See also *Sheffield Independent* for Saturday 26 September 1857; the *Manchester Guardian*, and the *London Evening Standard* on Friday 25 September 1857. It should be noted that the event took place before the Ground Game Act 1880 changed the law with regard to rabbits and hares.

out of her reckoning. A rabbit pounded for eating her cabbages would himself eat very nicely and pay dearly for his meal. However, it seems that there was hard by the garden and the fence a preserve, and where there is a preserve there is a keeper, and when a rabbit is caught in a trap you will not hinder it from screaming. Now the keeper beard a scream, which came from the rabbit in the snare, and saw the woman, spider-like, set off after her prey. The meeting was awkward, and unlike the spider, the female could not tangle herself in her web, and escape unnoticed. So the keeper told her she was doing wrong, the answer was that the vegetables were damaged, and the issue we suppose was a summons.

Thirty years later, in Ernest Dobson's Jubilee Year, there was another case in Wales, which was reported in the *Sheffield Evening Telegraph* for Monday 12 September 1887.

CAPTURE OF WOMEN POACHERS.

The Ruthin police have made a strange capture. Sergeant Evans and two constables having reason to suspect the home-coming a gang of well-known poachers, planted themselves the highway near the town, and when the men came along searched them without result. As it was obvious from the state of their clothes that they had been poaching the officers secreted themselves and were presently astonished to see three women crossing the fields to place where they remained some time. When they were returning the officers revealed themselves and insisted on searching them. Their intelligence was amply rewarded, for the ladies had slung twenty-seven rabbits on three strings, and tied them around their waists beneath their dresses, and in this way they were also carrying off two long lengths of rabbit netting. They protested that the protuberances were ordinary dress improvers, but the officers were obdurate, and at length the whole of the twenty-seven rabbits were produced. The women will be brought before the county magistrates charged with being in the illegal possession of game.

Five

Comparisons

Ernest Dobson was an habitual poacher, even as a youth. He went out during the night, at first to places close to home, in and around Scholes and Thorpe Hesley, but eventually further and further afield, in search of game – rabbits and hares, sometimes birds, but not fish or deer. Sometimes he went alone, sometimes in company; and in course of time, he became an old hand, who prided himself on the accuracy of his shooting.

Although his name never appeared in *The Times*, Dobson did make the (minor) headlines in local newspapers on numerous occasions. When he appeared before the court, he was generally described as Ernest Dobson of Thorpe Hesley (see under 1879, 1880, 1881, 1883, 1890, 1899, 1901, 1903, 1904 and 1905), but was sometimes said, or thought, to come from Scholes (1877 and 1878), Chapeltown (1887), Ecclesfield (1882) and Masbrough (1900). Now, these are all places in South Yorkshire and are near to one another, while Scholes was in the ecclesiastical parish of Thorpe Hesley, but in the civil parish of Kimberworth, while part of Thorpe Hesley was in Chapeltown and also in Ecclesfield, so that there plenty of scope for confusion; but, I did wonder whether he had sometimes deliberately misled the court about where he resided, in view of his use of an alias ('Slynn') in Chesterfield in 1896. I concluded, however, that he was probably telling the truth, firstly because the Censuses of 1861 and 1871 show him living in Scholes as a child, and secondly because he also told the court that he was a miner (in 1883, 1890, 1895, 1900, 1904) or collier (1879, 1881, 1891), or ripper (1901)[92], or labourer (1882, 1887, 1891, 1902, 1903, 1905); and these were all occupations which might well have required him to move around in search of work.

He did not always tell the truth about his previous convictions, or about his way of life. He knew that what was he doing was wrong, in fact criminal; but, as we know, he claimed that this was merely 'pot-poaching', which was 'not very bad'.

POACHING

In the early 19th century Justices of the Peace were prone to classify all those who appeared before them for breaches of the game laws as 'notorious poachers', just as they had at one time referred to a wide class of people as 'rogues and vagabonds'; and something of this attitude still remained in Ernest Dobson's day. He was certainly not the only persistent offender in his village. Numerous other offences of night poaching were committed by men from Thorpe Hesley, for example in 1858, 1864, 1867, 1868, 1870, 1874, and 1876; and, even when no prosecution was recorded, there were many occasions when the police visited Thorpe Hesley, after some poaching-related offence had been committed, because it was known that 'game trespass' was endemic there.

Dobson's own record begins in 1877; but the newspapers recorded several incidents prior to that date, which provide the context for his activities. The following report, with its comical exchange regarding a dog, appeared in the *Sheffield Independent* for Saturday 13 April 1844:

COURT-HOUSE, ROTHERHAM. MONDAY, April 8.
DEER STEALING.
PUNISHING THE DOG.

Wm. Moxon, a notorious poacher, of Thorpe Hesley, was charged on the information of Geo. Marsh Palmer, park-keeper to the Right Hon. Earl Fitzwilliam, with stealing a fallow-deer from

---

92 Ripper: a person who works in a mine, ripping out coal.

Wentworth Park. It appeared from the evidence of Mr. Palmer, and Edw. Emmerson, (constable of Wentworth,) that a fallow deer having been missed out of the park, a search-warrant, dated the 4th of April, was obtained, and the prisoner's house and premises were searched, and the carcase and the head of a fallow-deer were found concealed in a rabbit-hole adjoining. The offence was not charged as a felony, but under the 27th sec. of the 7th and 8th Geo. IV., c. 21.[93] The penalty on conviction was £20, or a committal to the House of Correction for not less than four, nor more than six calendar months, for non-payment.

The dog with which the offence was suspected to have been committed was produced. He was a fine animal, and well adapted for the purpose. A witness named Wm. Garnett was called, and owned the dog, but the animal seemed to recognise the prisoner as his master, in preference to any other party. Mr. Whitfield for the defence took objection that an information ought to have been taken out, setting forth the offence of which the defendant had been guilty, and the jurisdiction of the Magistrates to hear and determine upon it. The Magistrates, after hearing the objections, convicted the defendant in the full penalty of £20, and in default of payment he was committed for six calendar months.

On the restoration of the dog being applied for, Col. Fullerton asked tbe claimant how many hares he had caught in one night, belonging to Lord Wharncliffe? The man, of course, was not cognizant of the fact. The Magistrate said he had caught seventeen hares in one night, belonging to Lord Wharncliffe; adding, that more was known of the dog than the owner was aware of. The dog was detained.

Twenty years later the *Sheffield Independent* for Saturday 13 May 1865 noted no less than three incidents of poaching relating to Wentworth Park, the first and third being of interest because of the youth of the accused.

---

93 The Act of 1827.

The Jubilee Poacher

USING A DOG TO TAKE GAME.

Thomas Hoyland and George Hoyland, of Wombwell, and Alfred Sloy, of Wentworth, were summoned for unlawfully using a dog to take game. Mr. Whitfield prosecuted, and Mr. Edwards defended.[94] On the 23rd of April last, Mr. Smith, who resides at Harley, near Wentworth, saw the defendants crossing a field with three dogs. A hare was started, and one of the dogs followed, and killed it. The hare was taken up by witness, and the defendants walked away. For the defence, it was stated that some sheep belonging to one of the defendants had strayed, and while they were being driven back their dog broke from them, and pursued the hare. They neither sent it nor encouraged Sloy, who was only twelve years of age. Sloy was discharged, with the caution not to get into such a mess again. The other defendants were each fined £1 and costs.

AN OLD OFFENDER.

William Orvill was summoned for trespassing in pursuit of game. Mr. Whitfield prosecuted, and Mr. Hirst defended. On the 27th of April the defendant was seen by a gamekeeper named Lilly, in tbe service of Mr. Jubb, ranging with a terrier dog over a field at Wickersley in pursuit of game. Mr. Hirst called a witness to prove that the defendant went into the field in search of Mr. Shore, who owns a quarry in the field. It was denied that he was seeking game. Previous convictions were proved against the defendant, and he was fined 20s. and costs. George Young was summoned on the information of Joseph Scholey, gamekeeper in the service of Earl Fitzwilliam, for a similar offence. The defendant lived in a cottage in Wentworth Park, and on Sunday week be was seen to leave home with a lurcher dog. In a few moments a hare was put up, which the dog pursued and killed. The defendant, who did not appear, was fined 40s. and costs, or one month's imprisonment

---

94 In the late 1850s, Earl Fitzwilliam used the legal services of William Whitfield on a regular basis: see the Household Accounts in SCA, WWM A-176, 178, 180, 181.

UNPLEASANT TERMINATION TO AN EXCURSION.

Five lads, named respectively Arthur Shillito, George Evans, Thomas Pardoe, Henry Marshall, and Frederick Reed, from Parkgate, were summoned for trespassing in pursuit of game. Mr. Whitfield was for the prosecution. George Airey, gamekeeper in the service of Earl Fitzwilliam, stated that on Saturday morning the 22nd ult., he was on duty in Wentworth Park, when he saw the defendants walking near the water. Shortly afterwards after they went to the boat-house, and by some means broke the lock of the door and got out the boat. Three of them got into it, and they had a row on the water. They then drew to the back, and after walking about a while, they went to the stew pond and commenced snaring pike. He went up to them as they lay on the grass, and found they had caught eleven fish. He charged them with the offence, and they made no attempt to deny it. Mr. Whitfield said the defendants had rendered themselves liable to be indicted at the sessions for the offence, but on account of their youth it had been decided to have the case brought before the Bench for decision. The defendants pleaded guilty. Shillito, Evans, and Reed, who appeared to have been the leaders of the excursion, were each fined 20s. and costs, or fourteen days; Pardoe and Marshall were fined 5s. and costs, or one week

CRIMES OF VIOLENCE AND AFFRAYS

Involvement in poaching often involved further charges against the accused. Ernest Dobson's convictions were almost exclusively for poaching, and the great majority were for 'mere' poaching, but there were several for assault (1881, 1887, 1903) including assaults on gamekeepers and a policeman; and in 1890 he was charged with making threats to murder a gamekeeper, though he was acquitted when tried. He was never charged with affray – all the convictions for assault being 'one-on-one'. In this he was fortunate, firstly because he sometimes did go out poaching in company, and secondly because affrays were regarded by the courts as very serious matter, especially when they involved the death of, or injury to, a gamekeeper.

The Jubilee Poacher

Respectable society feared the armed gang; but at the same time the newspaper archives reveal that many gamekeepers were 'up for it', as we might say now – that they were not reluctant to fight the poachers, and indeed sometimes lay in wait for, and attacked them (for example in 1865, 1867, 1868, 1877 and 1898). John Wilkins of Essex devoted an entire chapter of his book to 'Poachers' Dogs and How to Kill Them' His philosophy was: 'shoot a good dog and the whole gang is broken up for the season.

Magistrates, juries and judges were quite prepared to condemn excessive violence, when they found evidence of it. We have already seen this in the Rotherham case of 1865, when William Lilly, gamekeeper on the Silverwood estate lost his life, but the jury brought in a verdict of manslaughter. There is a similar case from the same year (admittedly not involving homicide) which was the subject of both criminal and civil proceedings, where the outcome was very different.

The criminal proceedings at the Assizes in Leeds were reported in the *Sheffield Independent* for Wednesday 5 April 1865.

Three men named William Wilton, Uriah Nelson, and Joseph Beardshall, were indicted for night poaching, being armed, on the estate of Lord Wharncliffe. The case for the prosecution was as follows. On the night of the 11th December [1864] the head gamekeeper (Thirkill) of Lord Wharncliffe, and several other gamekeepers were on duty in a place called Tedd Springs, and about one o'clock in the morning they heard several shots fired. Proceeding in the direction of the sound, they saw the three prisoners approaching. Henry Thirkill (the keeper) challenged them, whereupon Nelson and Wilson called out to the other prisoner, who had a double-barrelled gun, to shoot, and Beardshall put the gun to his shoulder, but he did not fire. The keepers advanced upon them, and the prisoner Nelson, who was armed with a hedge-slasher, made a blow at the headkeeper with it, but Thurkill warded it off with his stick, and closed with Nelson (who is about half his size) knocked him down, and then took him into custody. Wilson ran away, but was captured; Beardshall made his escape for the time. The keepers found that

Nelson and Wilson were in possession of two dead pheasants, recently killed, a shot bag, the hedge-slasher, and a number of heavy stones. A few hours afterwards, Thirkill went to Beardshall's house at Brightside, with a policeman named French. When they knocked on the door, the prisoner and his wife opened a window, and whilst the keeper and the officer were entering the house, a dead pheasant was thrown out of the window. No gun was found in the house.

His Lordship said that usually cases of this description were disposed of before the magistrates; and he did wish - especially since the recent stringent but wholesome statute[95] had given them large powers in such cases - that they would (he was about to say) wash their dirty linen at home, in cases where keepers had done such things had been adverted to here. He wished that the magistrates would dispose of these poaching cases for themselves, except in cases where actual violence had been done by the poachers to the keepers. These cases ought to be sent to the assizes, in order that persons might learn that they must obey the law, and that they could not offer violence with impunity. However, this case had been sent here, and it must be dealt with according to law.

After stating that the prisoners had clearly been guilty of an infraction of the law, his Lordship said his summing up would not be complete if he did not allude to the force used by the keepers. Whatever effect that might have had upon the mind of the court in passing sentence, it had nothing whatever to with the issue the jury had to try. The simple question for them was, were these men night poachers? He begged to say it was clear that keepers, coming upon three more persons in the night, armed, poaching, might arrest those persons, and therefore the arrest of Wilson and Nelson, *qua* the arrest, was lawful; but with respect to the means used, he was equally bound to say they were not lawful.

A man had no right to shoot a dog that had bitten him if it was running away. On the evidence, it was clear that the keepers had no right to strike these men; and he believed that this case was another illustration of the truth of a definition which had been laid down by one of the great

---

95 The Poaching Prevention Act of 1862.

literary ornaments of the age (Kingsley), that a gamekeeper very often is poacher turned outside in, and a poacher a gamekeeper turned inside out. Subsequently the learned Judge sentenced Wilson and Beardshall to three months, and Nelson, who had been most injured by the keepers, to two months' imprisonment.

'The civil proceedings, arising from related events were reported in the *Leeds Mercury* for Saturday 22 April 1865.

DAMAGES AGAINST A GAMEKEEPER FOR ASSAULTING A POACHER.

At the Barnsley County Court, yesterday, the Judge (Mr. Marshall) decided the case of *Beardshaw v. Thirkell*, which for some time past has created more than usual interest in the district. The action was brought to recover £50 for assault under the following circumstances. The complainant, a fork grinder, of Brightside, near Sheffield, for years has been known as a poacher, and his son, aged about twenty-four years, has followed in his steps so far looking after game is concerned, whilst the defendant is head gamekeeper to Lord Wharncliffe, of Wortley Hall. On the morning of the 12th of December, the younger Beardshaw [sic] was taken from his father's house on the charge of night poaching. About two hours after, Thirkell, not being aware of the apprehension, went to the complainant's house, and (according to the testimony of several witnesses in support of the case, attacked Mrs. Beardshaw very savagely. She cried out for assistance, when the complainant got out of bed and ran downstairs to the kitchen, when Thirkell struck him with a life preserver, leaving him senseless. For the defence the defendant said he went to apprehend the younger Beardshaw, but instead of going into the house he sent in Police Constable Clegg. The constable stated that he went into the house, asked to look round to see if the young man charged with night poaching was there (not being aware of his apprehension), which was refused by Mrs. Beardshaw. Her husband (plaintiff) then came down and struck him, and had the blow returned. On cross-examination the constable admitted lending the defendant his staff some distance from the house of the plaintiff.

The Learned Judge, in delivering judgment, said that but for the previous character of the plaintiff, the case was of such a character as to demand heavy damages. There could not be a doubt but that the plaintiff had been most seriously injured, and had death resulted the defendant would have been guilty of manslaughter, if not of a much more serious offence. The plaintiff had been illegally and violently assaulted, and it ought to be known that the law would not permit a man to be knocked down by a gamekeeper because he was a poacher. With regard to the evidence of the police-officer, he hoped his conduct in the matter would be brought under the notice of Colonel Cobbe, the chief constable, and that it would be investigated.

The extraordinary sequel was that Thurkill was murdered, only two years later, by none other than Joseph Beardshall (or Beardshaw) junior! Reports of the affray appeared in numerous newspapers, including the *Manchester Courier and Hull Advertiser and Exchange Gazette;* the *Western Morning News*; and the *Sheffield Daily Telegraph*, all published on Friday 13 December 1867.

The facts were that a desperate encounter took place near Pilley—nine miles from Sheffield, and five from Barnsley—between a gang of poachers and a party of gamekeepers in the service of the Right Hon. Lord Wharncliffe of Wortley Hall.[96] The conflict resulted in the murder of one of the keepers and in the severe injury of another. It had been known to the keepers for some time that the neighbourhood was being frequently visited by poachers, and they have consequently exercised an increased degree of vigilance.

On the night in question, the watchers, convinced that they were unable to cope with formidable-looking a gang, sent, before discovering

---

96 Wortley Hall has belonged to trade unionists since 1951. It is still known as 'the Workers' Stately Home.'

themselves, for his lordship's head keeper, Mr. Thirkell. He promptly responded to the call, and came to the assistance of his men. No sooner did the keepers discover themselves than they were attacked by the poachers, and a short but murderous encounter followed. Mr. Thirkell attempted to seize one of the poachers, and while struggling with him another of the gang seized a gun, and at a distance of about four yards took aim and fired at him. The charge entered his abdomen and he fell and died almost immediately. He was not, we understand, even heard to speak after being shot.

The poachers, abandoning their nets, hastily made off in the direction of Thorpe Hesley. They also left behind them a hat and a walking-stick, but they took with them the gamekeeper's gun. Oram, one of the watchers, who was engaged in desperate struggle with one of the poachers, received a severe blow with a bludgeon and was partly disabled. The other watcher, Mayes, escaped without much injury. From the severe blows that were dealt the poachers by the keepers, it is believed that at least four of them have carried off broken heads.

A complete cordon was drawn round Rotherham, and had the murderers sought refuge in the immediate neighbourhood they must inevitably have been captured. Every house where it was known men of poaching proclivities were harboured was visited and a mental note taken the inmates, and hardly a soul was allowed to pass in the streets. In nearly every instance the petty poacher was found home in bed, but the more notorious of the fraternity were out of town, and there is reason to suppose that several of them were among the gang who fired the fatal shot at Thirkell. The parishes of Kimberworth, Scholes, Thorpe Hesley, Shiregreen, Ecclesfield, Chapeltown, Grimethorpe, Brightside, Attercliffe, and Carbrook were visited and revisited during a few hours, but, unfortunately, the parties looked for failed to return to their usual haunts; notwithstanding their cunning, however, there is hope they will soon be in the hands of the officers of the law. Arrests were duly made.

The story was taken up by numerous papers.[97] *The Durham Chronicle* for Friday 10 January 1868 provided valuable background information; and in particular that Joseph 'Beardshall' (see above), and Joseph 'Beardshaw' (or 'Bradshaw', or 'Beecher') (see below) were one and the same man.[98]

> On Thursday, Superintendent Ball, of the West Riding Constabulary, Bradford, received private information which led him to Littlebro', near Rochdale, where he succeeded in apprehending Joseph Bradshaw, alias Beecher, who was working in a brick yard there. Joseph English, whom suspicion points as having been the person who shot Thirkhill, was apprehended near Tuxford. He had been playing hide-and-seek ever since the affray, awaiting a favourable opportunity of getting out of the country. Both Bradshaw and English lived at Carbrook, Attercliffe Common, the former's occupation being that of pot-maker for steel smelters, and the latter's that of joiner. English was tried in 1861 for the murder of man named Crooks, in Thorpe Hesley, but he was acquitted; and at Leeds Assizes in March, 1865, Bradshaw, along with two others, was convicted of night poaching on the estate of Lord Wharncliffe at Wortley, and was sentenced to three months' imprisonment. Bradshaw's capture on that occasion was effected by the deceased gamekeeper, Thirkhill. A few years ago, Bradshaw's father brought an action against Thirkhill for trespass, and succeeded in recovering damages.

At the Assizes in Leeds, the Grand Jury found a true bill against Joseph English, Matthew Cutts, and Joseph Beardshaw, for the murder of Thirkell; but there was no bill found for the murder, so far as Joseph Gregory was concerned. However, true bills were found against Cutts, Beardshaw, Gregory, and English for misdemeanour. At the trial itself, before the 'petty' jury of 12, a preliminary point was taken by the

---

97 See the *York Herald*, Saturday 11 January 1868; the *Stamford Mercury*, Friday 31 January 1868; the *Rochdale Observer*, Saturday 22 February 1868; the *Yorkshire Post and Leeds Intelligencer*, Wednesday 18 March and Tuesday 24 March 1868; the *Bradford Observer,* Thursday 26 March 1868; *Sheffield Daily Telegraph*, Friday 27 and Saturday 27 March 1868; and the *Yorkshire Post and Leeds Intelligencer*, Monday 30 March 1868.
98

defence that Lord Wharncliffe had not been shown to have the right of preserving and killing game on the land in question; but this was quickly disposed of.

Mr. Smith, resident agent to the Right Hon. Lord Wharncliffe was called to prove the ownership of the land in question, but he was unable to give positive evidence that his lordship retained the right of preserving and shooting the game in the field in which Thirkell was killed, and which was in the occupation of Mr. Pearson. Mr. Dixon, the deputy-clerk of the peace for the West Riding, proved that Lord Wharncliffe is the Lord of the Manor of Pilley. The Hon. F. S. Wortley was then called as a witness and deposed that his brother was Lord of the Manor, and that he had seen him exercise the right of shooting over the estate. The "deputation" was then put in and read, and the Judge held that its authority was conclusive evidence on the point in issue.

Mr. Maule, having taken a bad point, then took a good one:

He remarked that Thirkell and those who were with him were engaged in the fulfilment of lawful duty, they were to be protected in the discharge of that duty, and that inasmuch the prisoners having caused his death, under those circumstances they were most certainly guilty of murder.

Mr. Blackburn, on behalf of Beardshaw, said

He would not seek to inflame the feelings the jury by speaking of the Game Laws and the evils attendant upon them, because, no doubt, as his lordship would tell them, so long as the Game Laws were the law of the land, whether good or bad, they must be respected. The learned counsel then explained the law of murder, showing that in this case it would be necessary in order to find the prisoners guilty, to prove that they had killed Thirkell with malice aforethought whilst engaged in unlawful occupation and unlawful means. He then put it to the jury whether, in solemn case like this, where men's lives hung on their decision, they ought to receive any but clear and reliable evidence. He submitted that, in order to justify a verdict of murder, there must be no doubt of the confederacy of these men, and there must be the clearest identity; but there were he said, elements that could not be found in this case. He urged that there was no conclusive evidence.

When it came to the summing up, the Judge said:

> [The jury] could take it from him that the keepers had a right to arrest these men, engaged, as they were, in poaching at that time. Now, these men set out with the intention of poaching, and if they conceived beforehand the intention making use deadly weapons, such as they had in their possession, in the event of their being obstructed in carrying out their intention poaching. If they intended to use these deadly weapons for the purpose of preventing their being arrested by those who had come for the purpose of arresting them, they would be guilty of murder, should death ensue from the use of those deadly weapons.

The jury decided otherwise. English and Cutts were acquitted of murder but found guilty of manslaughter. Beardshaw and Gregory were acquitted of murder but found guilty of poaching.

Following this, the judge referred to the 'merciful view' taken by the jury and said that, but for that, he would have sentenced all four prisoners to death. He proceeded to sentence English to ten years' penal servitude, Cutts to five years' penal servitude, Beardshaw to eighteen months' imprisonment, and Gregory to fifteen months' imprisonment with hard labour.

When we compare Ernest Dobson's career in crime with what we know of the Beardshaws, we may well conclude that both men were lucky to get off so lightly, in their encounters with gamekeepers; but we can also see what Dobson meant when he claimed that pot-poaching (not involving violence) was 'not very bad'. No doubt he would also have thought that when it came to a fight, the keepers gave as good as they got, and sometimes more.

The Jubilee Poacher

THE VIEW FROM THE BENCH

In Ernest Dobson's day Thorpe Hesley was not like D.H.Lawrence's fictional Tevershall - a 'terribly seething welter of ugly life, more like a central African jungle than an English village'; but nor was it the Utopian vision of rural harmony and contentment imagined by William Morris in his novel *News from Nowhere* (1890). In the early 20th century, it was still known as 'Mutton Town', because it had once had a reputation as the haunt of the sheepstealer;[99] and we have seen that it was also home to a number of poachers, including friend Dobson. However, when we consider the newspaper reports as a whole, Dobson was undoubtedly right to say that 'pot-poaching' was 'not very bad', compared with other sorts of local crime. Examples include sheep stealing (1840); poultry stealing (1842); highway robbery and theft of horses; robbery (1825 and 1844); cutting and maiming (1849); robbing a gunpowder magazine; alleged manslaughter by a midwife (1850); murder of a young woman by her rejected suitor (1855); stealing turnips (1858); a 'garotte' robbery (1863); unlawful possession of a gun (1867); and highway robbery (1870).

From a modern standpoint, it is all too easy to romanticise poaching, just as some have romanticised the activities of medieval outlaws, 'primitive rebels', 18th century highwaymen and modern train-robbers; but what did the magistrates and judges of the time (who knew the facts in detail) think of Ernest Dobson? Did they accept his excuse that what he did was not very serious?

The answer is no. The magistrates knew Dobson as 'the Jubilee Poacher', a name he had acquired almost twenty years previously with numerous convictions since, not only for poaching but for assault, including assaults on gamekeepers and police officers (1881, 1882, 1887 & 1903), criminal damage (1877 & 1893) 'indecency' (1902), being drunk (1881) and using obscene language (1906). Moreover, long before 1905, the prosecutors knew that Dobson was undoubtedly

---

99 The late Robert Chesman wrote [p.5] "Thorpe once had a nickname – 'Mutton Town'. In 1893 the village "Bobby" had been warned to look out for rustlers in Thorpe. Being on friendly terms with many inhabitants he called on one in Hesley Lane. He expressed surprise at seeing a cradle near the hearth and remarked that he didn't know about any new arrival. "Well", was the reply, "you know what t' neighbours are like i' Thorpe, so we've not talked about it much". After chatting for a time the policeman took his leave but in doing so disturbed the cradle - and its occupant - which turned out to be a lamb!

more than just an occasional 'pot-poacher'. At least one lawyer stated publicly that Dobson was a professional (or at least habitual) poacher, whose activities enabled him [the lawyer] to earn a tidy income from his appearances in court, prosecuting game-related offences! Moreover, the magistrates probably suspected that Dobson's official record was the tip of a substantial iceberg.

Before we examine the question of whether Dobson made a profit as a poacher, it is worth pointing out that he confined himself to shooting ground game and birds, and to netting the former; and does not seem to have gone after deer or fish, athough this may be explained by virtue of the fact that in the local area, fish were probably only available in the Lakes inside Wentworth Park, which may have been difficult to penetrate undetected.

One thing is certain. Whether or not they accepted Dobson's excuse, the magistrates' powers of sentencing were limited in the late 19th century. By this time justice had been deprived of the 'terrors' which the *Quarterly Review* had mentioned in 1820. Capital punishment and transportation had been consigned to the dustbin of history, along with spring-guns and mantraps. The courts were left with the power to fine, or imprison for default, and this was not a deterrent, so far as Dobson was concerned. There was therefore little the courts could do with 'inveterate poachers'; and this may account for some of the ferocity shown by gamekeepers towards their opponents in the 1880s and '90s.[100]

Whatever drove him, Ernest Dobson was strongly motivated. He was prepared to run the risk of frequent arrest and imprisonment. He was also prepared for violence, for gamekeepers and poachers each carried sticks and guns, and were prepared to use them. There is also some evidence of this in his changing appearance over the years. When he was admitted to the prison in Wakefield in 1883, he was found to have a 'blue cut on [his] left eyebrow', though in 1890 he had 'several small moles on [his] neck [and a] mole above [his] left eyebrow'. In 1891 he was described as having a 'small moles on [his] right cheekbone' and moles 'on [his] neck and left hand arm'. Nothing sinister there one may think, but later in the same year he was said to have a 'cut on [the] bridge of [his] nose.' In 1896, the authorities in Wakefield found that he had a 'large cut mark [on the]

---

100 In August 1885 the *Illustrated Sporting and Dramatic News* ran an article entitled 'How we got rid of an inveterate poacher'; but it turned out to be about the shooting of a hen harrier in Ireland.

right side [of his] forehead, though admittedly, no distinguishing marks at all were noted in 1899, 1905 or 1906.

POACHING FOR PROFIT?

It is unlikely that Ernest Dobson saw himself as engaged in a sort of class war, though this is how James Harker saw it. Dobson's 'victims' included several aristocrats but also industrial enterprises like Newton Chambers, tenant farmers like Joseph Cooper of Scholes, and others who owned shooting rights. Some of these men were Dobson's neighbours or near neighbours; and the fighting took place between poachers and gamekeepers, who were workers too.

It is unlikely that Ernest Dobson poached in pursuit of fame or notoriety. According to a report in the *Sheffield Independent* in 1890, the court was told that he knew that he was called "the Jubilee Poacher", but the prosecution 'was not able to say if [he] was proud of the fact'. The soubriquet may even have been a hindrance because, presumably, the more famous he became, the more likely he was to be apprehended.

Did he do it for the money? There was a difference between poaching for one's own table, and poaching for commercial purposes. The former might be regarded as petty crime, similar to stealing turnips; but there must have been some poachers in South Yorkshire who hunted game for profit. Such men may have been encouraged and assisted by the development of the railways, which made it easier to send game to various markets, and by the invention of the breech-loading gun in the 1860s and '70s, which increased the amount which could be 'bagged' several fold.[101]

James Harker tells us that he became a poacher because he and his family were poor, and he stayed a poacher because he could make extra money that way. He could sell three hares for 12 shillings,[102] and he could shoot a great many hares in a single night:

> As soon as I got my Gun, I made Good use of it. In two years I shot 300 hares Besides what I assisted in Killing with others in nets. To show you

---

101 Chenevix Trench, 166, 171.
102 Harker, 31.

how I Troubled the Game-preserving Class, I was Fined £8 for Killing Hares. So I Flew away and the Debt still stands. I was fined £3 for Killing Hares another time, 5 pounds for killing without a Licence.

Clearly Harker made a profit; and one of the lawyers who prosecuted Ernest Dobson told an exasperated court in May 1890 that "by a night's poaching they [Dobson and his confederates] could easily obtain money to pay any fine magistrates could inflict upon them". However, there were major differences between the two men. Dobson usually gave his occupation as 'miner' or 'collier', so that (so far as we know) he had the opportunity of profitable work throughout his adult life. The journalists never described him as a 'pauper', a term which they ready to use in appropriate cases. His earnings as a coalminer may have been as much as £1 per week. On the other hand, employers in his day could dictate terms and conditions, and work was far from regular in the mining industry. In addition, Dobson may have found it difficult to find work, given the evil reputation which he acquired in his youth, with local landowners and employers alike; and the fact that by 1900, he was already regarded as old.

Unlike Harker, Dobson was frequently arrested, and often appeared in court, usually for game offences, but sometimes for crimes of violence, and on one occasion for indecency. The consequence was that he was fined very frequently, and spent several years in prison overall. This must have been very disruptive since, when he was in prison, he was not earning at all. As for his income from poaching, we do not know how much he could get for a rabbit or hare; but the fact that he generally chose not to pay fines, and go to prison instead, suggests that he had little or no money, most of the time.

On the whole I am inclined to think that the reason Ernest Dobson continued to poach so persistently and so frequently was love of the sport, and the recreation it brought. 'Sport' was one of the reasons Harker gave for continuing to poach all his life; and love of I was also one of the reasons an MP gave, for his opposition to the Prevention of Poaching Act of 1862: he thought that Englishmen would continue to hunt, whatever legal obstacles lay in their way. Ernest Dobson used the word himself, when he told the magistrates in 1892 "It's only for a bit of sport in a day time. I've never been a night poacher in my life".

The Jubilee Poacher

(He also told them that he 'seldom missed when he put his gun to his shoulder').

Dobson was born and brought up in Scholes, which was a place where the fields and woods were all around him [see illustration 1], but it had a coal-mine, while several pits were sunk in and around his second home in Thorpe Hesley, during his lifetime. It was at this time also that ironworks, blast furnaces, engineering workshops and factories were built or re-built at Elsecar and Thorncliffe [see illustrations 5, 6 & 9]. Poaching was a way of enjoying the countryside; and, for a miner, it was also a way of enjoying the sun on his back, or at least the wind and the rain in his hair. Perhaps it was also a habit, like drinking and smoking, which he found it difficult to give up.

Appendix I: Nets

Long nets enabled the poacher to take ground game – rabbits and hares especially – on an almost industrial scale. James Harker tells us that he once was present when he and his companions caught 188 rabbits and 3 hares in Salcey Forest, Crown land seven miles from Northampton. He describes the technique as follows

Long nets are of different lengths. If you are going to work with a Party, a net 75 yards long may be enough. If you have one a 100 yards long, you would have to do more work During the night and only take your share of the spoil. But if you Lived and Worked a good deal by yourself has I have, the Longer your net the Better.

When six men are going out with a net 75 yards long, number one poacher peggs his net Down at the Start with a Short iron peg. Then away you all go in Front of the wood or spinney. When number one has run his net out 75 yards, Pull it rather Tight and Stick another iron peg in the ground to keep it so. There the net Lays Ready for Pegging up with Eight Long Pegs you have in a Long Coat Pocket.

Now you begin to peg it up. As you do this the other five men go and Do the same. The net when set would be forty inches high or more, according to a man's taste. There would be 75 yards of line top and bottom and if a good net, 120 yards of netting- if the net was tight and lacking what we call Bagging or Loose netting. If it was not Baggy, the net would not kill. Prey would hit against it and Bounce Back, but when they strike the loose net, the Bagging covers them and the more they struggle the worse' for them. They are killed by Feeling,' as I have said before.

Appendix II: Guns

My friend John Addy informs me that guns come in two kinds: shotguns and rifles. Shotguns are especially useful for the poacher, because they discharge lead shot across a wide area, and so can be used to shoot ground game, especially rabbits – which tend to run about – and also to shoot birds on the wing. Nowadays, an air-rifle is often used, because this is largely silent; but it is only effective at relatively short range. It is likely that a 19th century poacher would have found it useful in theory to take along a rifle, since birds roost at night, and then they are still; but again, the poacher may not have been able to afford both types of weapon; and the first mass-produced air rifle was only marketed in 1888. Dobson's weapon of choice would therefore (most likely) have been a shotgun; but, on the other hand, poachers did not always follow the rules.

Abbreviations & Sources

ABBREVIATIONS
ACM: Arundel Castle Manuscripts
BNA: The British Newspaper Archive www.britishnewspaperarchive.co.uk
DD: Drake's Directory of Rotherham, 1862
SCA: Sheffield City Archives
WD: White's Directory of Sheffield and Twenty miles around, 1891
WWM: Wentworth Woodhouse Muniments

PRIMARY SOURCES
Ancestry.co.uk for information derived from parish registers, censuses and prison registers
Drake's Directory of Rotherham, 1862
White's Directory of Sheffield and Rotherham, 1891
Doncaster Archives: Wentworth Parish Registers and Ecclesiastical Records
Grace's Guide to British Industrial History
Rotherham Central Library, Archives and Local Studies Section; Manor of Kimberworth Court Rolls: Parker Rhodes Collection 101 C 7; Kimberworth Enclosure Award and Act 1796-1800
Sheffield City Libraries, Archives Department: Fairbank Collection ERO 74 L; Ecc 104 S; Kimberworth and Wentworth Enclosure Act 1814: NBC 382 W 5; Kimberworth and Wentworth Enclosure Award 1821: NBC 62
West Yorkshire Archive Service, Wakefield: Deposited Turnpike Plans: R 161; Turnpike Annual Accounts: QE 22/84

Secondary Sources

An Old Ecclesfield Diary 1775 - 1845, ed. Thomas Winder (J.W. Northend Ltd, Sheffield, 1921)

Baines's *Directory of Yorkshire*, 1822

Charles Chenevix Trench *The Poacher and the Squire* (Longmans, 1967)

Chesman, J.R., *Thorpe Hesley, Its Past, Present and Future* (Hope Methodist Church, Thorpe Hesley, 1987)

Colegate, Isabel, *The Shooting Party* (Penguin Modern Classics, 1987)

Cooper, Stephen, *A House Divided: A House Divided, The Life and Death of John Billam of Thorpe Hesley*, (Bridge Publications, 1987)

Cooper, Stephen, *Flower Shows, Fraudsters & Horrible Murders, The Secret Journal of Aaron Allott* (published on chivalryandwar.co.uk)

Drinkall, Margaret, *Murder & Crime in Rotherham*, (*The History Press*, 2010)

Drinkall, Margaret, *Rotherham Murders*, (*Pen & Sword*, Barnsley, 2011)

Gummer, Alderman George, *Reminiscences of Rotherham* (Rotherham, H. Garnett & Co. Ltd., 1927)

Harker, James, *James Harker's Journal, A Victorian Poacher*, ed. Garth Christian (Oxford University Press, 1978)

Hey, David, *The Making of South Yorkshire* (Moorland Publishing, 1979)

Hey, David, *Yorskhire from AD 1000* (Longman, 1986)

Hines, Barry, *The Gamekeeper* (Michael Joseph, 1975, Penguin, 1979)

Hopkins, Harry, *The Long Affray* (Secker & Warburg, London, 1985)

Jones, Melvyn, *South Yorkshire Mining Villages* (Pen & Sword, Barnsley, 2017)

Mee, Graham: *Aristocratic Enterprise. The Fitzwilliam Industrial Undertakings* 1795 - 1857, Blackie, 1975

Other Books by Stephen Cooper

available from Amazon
or on www.chivalryandwar.co.uk)

A House Divided (Bridge Publications, 1987)

Burglars and Sheepstealers, (chivalryandwar.co.uk, 1992)

Sir John Hawkwood (Pen & Sword, 2008)

Sir John Fastolf (Pen & Sword, 2010)

Agincourt, Myth & Reality (Pen & Sword, 2014)

Earl Fitzwiliam's Treasure Island (with John Moorhouse, CreateSpace, 2016)

Cocos Island and the Treasure of Lima (CreateSpace, 2017)

Flowers Shows, Frauds and Horrible Murders (chivalryandwar.co.uk, 2017)

Illustrations

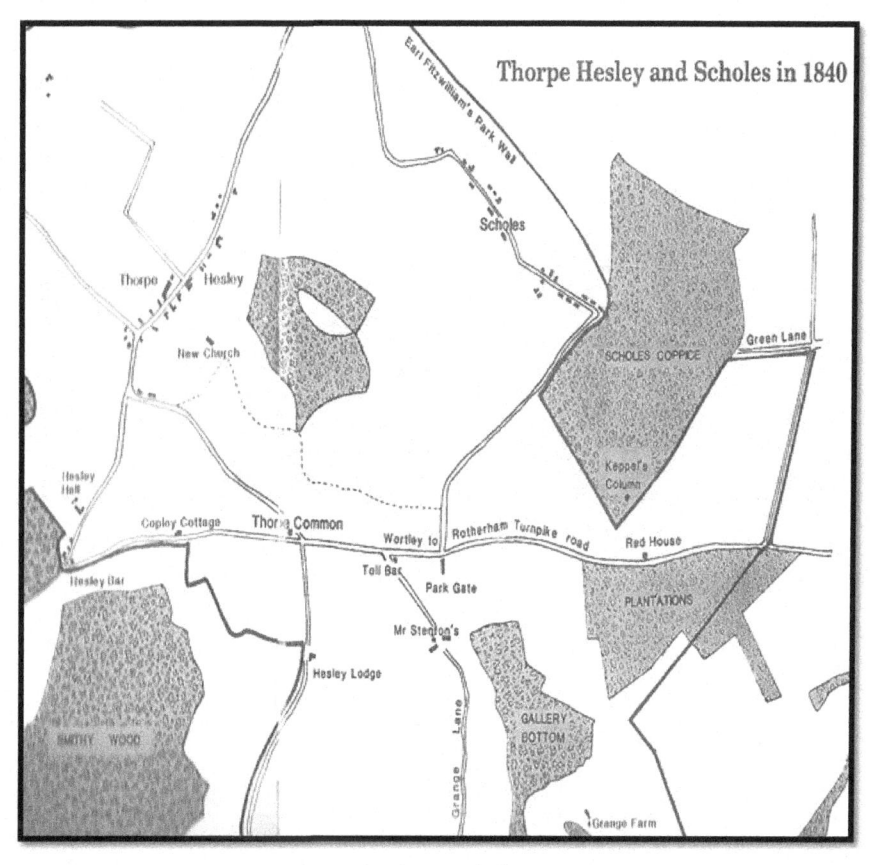

1 Thorpe Hesley & Scholes, c. 1840

2 Wentworth Woodhouse, 2017

The Jubilee Poacher

3 Wentworth from Thorpe Hesley Recreation Ground, 2017

4 The Rockingham Mausoleum, by Paul Caton, 2017

The Jubilee Poacher

5 Powerhouse Square, New Yard, Elsecar Workshops, 2017

6 The Dove and Dearne canal basin. Elsecar

The Jubilee Poacher

7 Elsecar by the Sea

8 Mangham's in Scholes

The Jubilee Poacher

9 Thorncliffe Ironworks

10 Hesley Hall, Hesley Lane, 2017

The Jubilee Poacher

11 The Red Lion

12 A Pub Outing

The Jubilee Poacher

13 The Ball Inn

14 The former Mechanics' Institute, 2017

The Jubilee Poacher

15 Old Methodist Chapel, Thorpe Street, and Sunday School, 1905

Stephen Cooper

16 New Methodist Chapel, Thorpe Street

The Jubilee Poacher

17 Barley Hall & Farm

Stephen Cooper

18 Thorpe Pit

The Jubilee Poacher

19 Gamekeepers & Poachers, 1885

20 Gamekeeper and Poacher, 1912